DEEP WEALTH

AN EXPLORATION OF MONEY, MEANING AND
WHAT REALLY MATTERS

Chad S. Hamilton, CFP®

PFI Publishing
DENVER, CO

PFI Publishing
3544 Yosemite St.
Denver, CO 80238
www.PlanForImpact.com

Cover Design by Creatiff Design
Author Photograph by Ginny Rutherford Photography

Ordering Information:
Quantity sales. Special discounts are available on quantity purchases by corporations, associations, and others. For details, contact the "Special Sales Department" at the address above.

Deep Wealth/Chad Hamilton —1st ed.
ISBN 978-0615817385

Contents

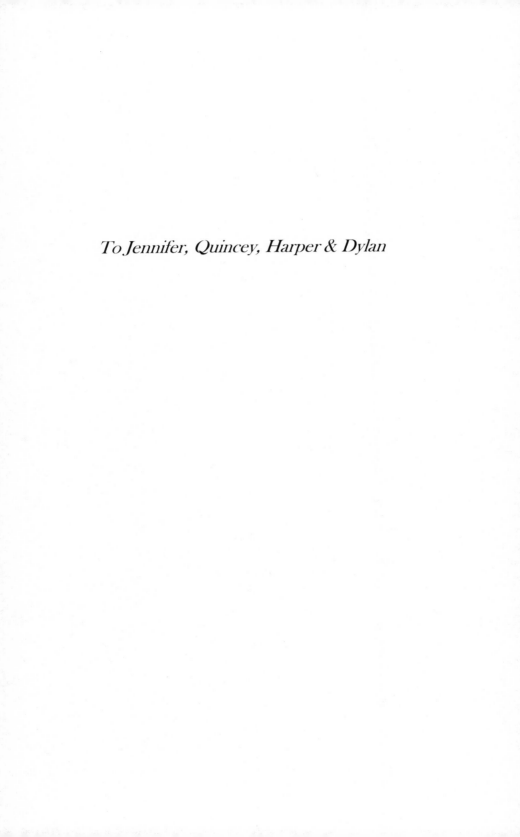

To Jennifer, Quincey, Harper & Dylan

"We are half-hearted creatures, fooling about with drink and sex and ambition when infinite joy is offered us, we are like ignorant children who want to continue making mud pies in a slum because we cannot imagine what is meant by the offer of a vacation at the sea. We are far too easily pleased."

—C. S. Lewis[1]

Introduction

Deep Wealth /dēp welTH/: *A great amount or abundance extending far beneath the surface*

We are living in the most prosperous nation in the history of the world. After adjusting for inflation, the average standard of living in the U.S. is ten times greater than it was 90 years ago. To make this statistic more relatable, imagine that your income is immediately multiplied by ten. What would happen to your own financial situation? Would it improve? Would you pay off debts/increase savings?

The answers might seem obvious. Yes, indebtedness should decrease as financial capital increases. But in the realm of money, reality is anything but obvious. Over that same time period in which the U.S. standard of living increased ten-fold, the amount of debt each American owes increased twenty-fold.

There are myriad statistics that signify this problem. Two-thirds of families are only one paycheck away from financial hardship. The average sixty year-old has saved enough to provide only a few hundred dollars of monthly income in retirement. The average household carries more than $8000 of credit card debt. Personal bankruptcies have doubled in the last decade. And so on.

So what's the problem? Do we need more financial education?

Dalbar, Inc. is perhaps the preeminent market research company in the financial services industry. In 2014, the company released its 20th annual investor behavior analysis. Here is a synopsis of their findings:[2]

> *"Attempts to correct irrational investor behavior through education have proved to be futile. The belief that investors will make prudent decisions after education and disclosure has been totally discredited."*

So, educational efforts have been "futile." But it's not for a lack of effort. In the same study, Dalbar refers to *"enormous efforts by thousands of industry experts to educate millions of investors"* that have been "ineffective." If you search Amazon.com for personal finance books, you will discover nearly 58,000 options. But google "does financial education work" and you will quickly discover dozens of articles citing evidence to the contrary.

This all begs the question as to WHY financial education has not worked. Part of the answer has to do with the flawed premise of traditional economic theory.

Traditional economics assumes that each of us thinks and chooses unfailingly well... We think like Albert Einstein, store as much memory as an Intel mega-chip, and exercise the willpower of Mahatma Gandhi.

Traditional economics says it can never be a bad thing to have more choices. And that would be true if we were robotically rational in our decision making. But the reality is that we are driven largely by emotions. Therefore, we can benefit greatly by reducing the number of choices, thereby eliminating certain temptations.

The corrective offered to traditional economic theory has been the introduction of behavioral economics. The objective of behavioral economics is primarily to prevent us from getting into mistakes in the first place.

Behavioral economics argues that we need self-control strategies and automation to overcome emotional sabotage of our best-laid plans. Sometimes it is best to cut up credit cards, establish auto savings plans, and set a limit to the number of shopping trips. It's similar to proven research showing that if you'd like to lose weight, you should buy smaller plates and smaller packages of what you like.

Behavioral economics offers useful advice for all of us, but it is only part of the answer. It is a tool to help to save us from ourselves. It doesn't actually address the bigger issue going on.

In his book, *Stewardship*, Peter Block contends:[3]

> *"For us as individuals, our purpose gets deflected from what matters to what works. The intensity of the question 'How?' is an expression of having surrendered some part of ourselves, our own struggle with purpose and destiny, by constantly kneeling at the altar of expedience."*

Block is saying that we are far too concerned with questions of "how," and because of that we care too much about getting the right recipe, formula, steps to solve our problems. Yet, we care far too little about what we are actually trying to achieve and why it matters to us.

We live in a world filled with distractions. Because of this, we tend to operate on the surface. Practicality and efficiency rules the day and is the default modus operandi. Thanks to technological advances, we are always connected to work, social networks, news, or whatever we choose. Of course, there are advantages to this, but one big disadvantage is that important questions get pushed out by all the lesser ones more urgently vying for attention.

Ken Dychtwald, CEO of Age Wave research consultancy firm, concluded:[4]

> *"A lot of people kind of wander into retirement without having thought about it at all."*

How does this happen? It has to do with means and ends. In a nutshell, we often take the ends as a given and focus exclusively on the means to get there. We do this by concentrating on how to reach certain goals with precious little attempt to really understand and define the nature of the goals themselves. We end up very heavy on the "how" and very light on the "what" and "why."

Unfortunately, most financial advisors have not figured this out either. In a recent survey by Merrill Lynch,[5] 85% of people that work with a financial professional said they hadn't had a conversation with their advisor about their "hopes and dreams" for retirement.

There are two very different types of questions of equal importance: 1) Fact-Finding questions which focus on "what you have" and 2) Discovery questions about "what you believe."

An example of a fact-finding question is "When do you want to retire?" A discovery question on this topic would be "How do you visualize life in retirement?" The first question is important to know, but it's not meaningful without understanding the answer to the second question. Likewise, "Have you taken steps to reduce taxes at your death?" is good but insufficient. "How do you want to be remembered?" is the question that needs to be addressed first and foremost.

So why doesn't financial education work? Why do most financial plans sit on a shelf and gather dust? It is because we look for mathematical solutions to behavioral issues.

Without the motivation to act, no amount of logic and number-crunching will change a thing. If the discovery questions – the questions that get to the heart of who you are and what you care about – are not addressed, the results will be disappointing.

We're obsessed with getting from point A to point B without stopping to really understand and consider what point B actually looks like or why it's even important to us.

And what about point B? How should we be thinking about our hopes and dreams? You might think that our goals are too big; that we are in this financial mess due to the collective pursuit of unaffordable aspirations. Millions of people expected to accumulate riches through little more than positive thinking and negative saving. We need to "right-size" our desires, right? Be more realistic about what we want?

Ironically, it's the opposite problem. Our dreams are too small. It is little dreams that distract us and cause us to endlessly chase after life's toys or experiences in a futile attempt to fill the void. The fact is these little dreams are not capable of truly satisfying and fulfilling us. But we will try. We may even spend money we don't have. Or we may be frugal and do the right things in order to accumulate wealth, only to be unsatisfied and never have "enough."

When it comes down to it, you really have one of two options:

You can use your life to make money. (Chase little dreams)

OR

You can use your money to make a life. (Follow big dreams)

One thing is for sure. Far too many of us have it backwards. We spend our lives trying to make money - obsessing about it, worrying about it, fighting about it.... While far fewer of us really connect with a deeper passion and purpose in life and then figure out how to best utilize money to accomplish it.

There is no need for a sophisticated understanding of the mechanics of modern portfolio theory in order to grasp the basics of success in personal finance. The foundational concept is pretty simple and intuitive: spend less than you earn. We know that and we intend to follow that axiom. But the road to hell is paved with good intentions. Whether it is attributable to laziness, procrastination, or competing priorities, the problem is an inability to take action.

So how do we overcome inertia and spur on action? By forming a compelling vision of life after our goals are met. This book has a pretty simple premise: internal desires drive external behavior. But if that is true, it has radical implications for personal finances and investment management.

The French writer Antoine de Saint-Exupery famously said:

> *"If you want to build a ship, don't summon people to buy wood, prepare tools, distribute jobs, and organize the work, rather teach people the yearning for the wide, boundless ocean."*

It's important to understand that a ship is not the same as a rowboat. If you want to build a rowboat, you can do so by simply collecting the proper materials (wood and tools), giving basic instructions, and organizing the right people and plan. However, a ship is a much bigger and more massive undertaking. It involves a much greater commitment of time and energy and often takes several years to complete.

Nearly 100 years ago, when Saint-Exupery uttered those words, transoceanic air travel had not yet been attempted. Sea-faring was the dominant method to see the world. He was saying that to build a ship, you didn't just collect materials and people and tell them to make it happen. You needed to instill in those people a vision with a grand purpose that united and excited the group to do whatever it needed to do to make the vision a reality.

Martin Luther King Jr. mobilized millions and changed the culture of our nation. The catalyst was his "I Have a Dream Speech." As the author Simon Sinek has pointed out,[6] it was not called "I Have a Plan Speech." Plans are practical but do not inspire. Dreams, on the other hand, connect us with our values and a deeper yearning. As a result, they have the capacity to truly transform us.

This is a book about money. But it's also about much more than that. For too long, we have lived under the illusion that we can live in happy, neatly partitioned lives with "life management" residing in one room and "investment management" in another.

Every one of us has a complicated relationship with our money. Our problems are more behavioral than intellectual. And yet, we are unable to change behavior by merely focusing on behavior or a list of "how-to" instructions. We need to first address the *causes* of our behavior which are driven by our dreams and desires; grounded in the stories that we believe.

All of us have stories that we live by. These stories simplify and explain the world for us. They enable us to make financial decisions in a highly complex world.

In Section I (Human Capital), we will explore our own money stories by considering a number of key questions to determine what we believe about the nature of wealth, the purpose of work, and the meaning of retirement. We will then look at the implications of those beliefs and consider how they affect our passion, purpose, and potential.

Then, in Section II (Spiritual Capital), we'll unpack what we actually believe money will do for us. We tell ourselves we will be secure if we have at least a certain amount of money, we'll be free if we can save enough, we'll be loved or admired if we use our money in a certain way, or we'll be respected if we make enough money. Though we may be largely unaware of them, these subconscious beliefs are highly influential in our decision-making.

Once we have examined the nature of our beliefs, desires, and money stories in the first half of the book, we turn to more practical questions about reaching those goals: What specifically do you need to do to meet your goals and realize your aspirations? (Section III - Financial Capital)

Finally, in Section IV called "Social Capital", we'll wrestle with the idea of "the bigger story" – beyond ourselves – and how that can shape the impact we ultimately hope to have on the larger world. This can involve future generations, the local community, and/or the world. In short, this is the idea of legacy. What legacy do you want to leave?

Ultimately, we need to develop integrated money stories that reflect what's truly important to us and what inspires us. Then we will develop and follow a plan that allows us to reach our goals and our dreams. This is an exploration of money, meaning, and what really matters. It's a search for Deep Wealth.

Section I

HUMAN CAPITAL: "The Seed"

"A rock pile ceases to be a rock pile the moment a single man contemplates it, bearing within him the image of a cathedral." – Antoine de Saint-Exupery

[1]

Making Sense of Life

The children's show Sesame Street was built on the premise that if you can hold the attention of children, you can educate them. So, the producers of the show wanted to figure out exactly how to grab and hold the attention of young children.

What the creators of the show discovered early on was that children would only watch if they could make sense of what they were seeing. In one experiment, some researchers edited an episode so that several of the key sketches were out of order. They found that the kids stopped watching. This finding was – and is – far from obvious for most of us.

Typically, we think that it's the entertainment and stimulation that is of primary interest to kids when it comes to TV viewing. But in the experiments, the flash, dazzle, and animated puppets were all still there. It didn't matter though. The children would not bother watching a show if they could not make sense of what they were looking at.

In his book *The Tipping Point*, Malcolm Gladwell cited this study and concluded:[1] "Kids don't watch when they are stimulated and look away when they are bored. They watch when they understand and look away when they are confused."

If you think about it, it starts to make sense. Pre-school children begin asking a certain three letter word at some point and, once they start saying it, they seem to never stop. That word is "why."

As adults we are really no different. We incessantly try to make sense of life in various ways. We ask "why?" in the face of injustice and personal loss. Studies of bereavement have continually found that people who recover the quickest from the death of a loved one are those who can find some meaning in their loss. On the other hand, traumas that cause prolonged stress tend to be those that we cannot make sense of. Tragedies that seem completely random or meaningless are profoundly troubling.

We also search for meaning in our daily lives and interactions. The meaning we attribute to things, which forms our underlying expectations and beliefs, has an enormous potential to bring about change.

James Allen wrote a little book called *As a Man Thinketh*. In it, he states:[2]

> *"Mind is the master power that moulds and makes, and man is mind, and evermore he takes the tool of thought, and shaping what he wills, brings forth a thousand joys, a thousand ills. He thinks in secret and it comes to pass: environment is but his looking-glass."*

Allen wrote those words more than 100 years ago so this is not a new idea. However, the implications of this idea are nowhere near being fully understood.

Perhaps the most obvious example of this is found in what has been called the placebo effect.

A placebo is a substance or procedure which a patient accepts as a medicine or therapy but which has no specific therapeutic value. A placebo effect occurs when a patient's symptoms are alleviated in some way by a "treatment," which works entirely because an individual is *expecting* or *believing* that it will work. The placebo effect is powerful. In a study carried out at the University of Harvard, its effectiveness was tested in a wide range of disturbances, including pain, arterial hypertension and asthma.

The results were impressive. Consistently 30 to 40% of the patients obtained relief with the use of placebo. In countless other experiments over the years, the placebo effect has continued to effectively work in roughly 1/3 of all cases. As you can imagine, this has been a nuisance for pharmaceutical companies testing new drugs. They don't know if their new drugs work because they actually have real medicinal value or if they "work" merely due to the belief in the minds of test patients that they will be healed or cured.

A natural follow up question is how do the actions of the unconscious mind produce these physical symptoms? Instinctively, we want to know "is it real or just in your head?" But does it matter? Is the healing any less "real" if its origin is in the mind rather than more tangible, physical sources?

Consider the following story which comes from neuroscientist V.S. Ramachandran in his fascinating book, *Phantoms in the Brain.*[3]

A woman sat in a doctor's office grinning in anticipation of a long-awaited birth. Money was tight and, therefore, until that point, she had only been informally checked out by a midwife down the street. However, she decided it was time to see a doctor after she had felt the baby kicking for some time and was convinced labor was about to begin.

She showed all the typical signs of a woman nearly nine months pregnant. Her abdomen was vastly enlarged. She had stopped menstruating, started lactating, and had morning sickness. Yet, the doctor discovered she was missing one major sign and it was a biggy. There was no baby!

While rare, this is not an isolated incident. The condition is called pseudocyesis and generally occurs in women who desperately want to be pregnant. Consider the startling effects the mind has on a woman's body in cases like this. It exemplifies the actual transformative power behind the concept of "mind over matter."

In *Clinical and Experimental Hypnosis*, W.S. Kroger explained the physiology behind this type of physical transformation:[4]

> *"If a suggestion becomes a conviction, it has the power to produce an appropriate response in the body... it is known that thoughts based on conviction can heal or kill."*

We already mentioned the healing power of the placebo effect that has been consistently documented over the last fifty years. Victor Frankl, a psychologist and concentration camp survivor, shared a personal anecdote that illustrates the opposite effect.

In *Man's Search for Meaning*, Frankl tells the story of a man in the concentration camp with him who was convinced the war would end on March 30, 1945. As that date approached, it became clear that the war was not coming to an end. On March 29, the man fell ill. Two days later, he died.[5]

Frankl's account is consistent with the findings of Dr. George Engel, professor of psychiatry at the University of Rochester Medical Centre whose research showed *"extreme feelings of hopelessness and help-lessness produced sudden death."* This is perhaps most clearly seen in the numerous cases of psychogenic death that have been reported throughout the world.

Psychogenic death refers to death triggered by psychic stimuli. It's a situation in which a person is seriously distressed and believes there is no way out and feels completely helpless. The extreme helplessness in such cases leads to physical death. It points to the idea that people *literally* need hope in order to live.

The point is this: We cannot underestimate the importance of what we believe.

If our thoughts and convictions have power over our physical health (potentially even over life and death), they certainly can affect other facets of life such as relationships, ability to succeed, and overall well-being.

Margaret Thatcher cautioned,

> *"Watch your thoughts for they become words, watch your words for they become actions, watch your actions for they become your habits, watch your habits for they become your character, watch your character for it becomes your destiny."*

Philosophers have long acknowledged that it is not the objective world that influences us, but rather how we represent and interpret the world. Consider again the placebo. In most cases, it's a sugar pill. It has no healing ability contained within it. And yet, it is given a "meaning." For those patients who are healed after being treated with a placebo, it is much more than what it appears on the surface. It has a much larger presence. It is attributed with the power to heal.

This is not unlike the larger meanings we regularly attribute to symbols. Consider the U.S. flag. On one level, it is merely three colors of fabric woven together. It is just cloth material that is typically not even worth much. And yet it is much more than that. To the military veteran, it was worth risking his own life to defend. To the immigrant, it is the symbol of opportunity and hope. To nearly all Americans, it stirs some proud feelings of independence and freedom. To enemies of the U.S., it may symbolize decadence and imperialism. But one thing is for certain: it means much, much more than the mere fabric it is printed on. We make it so.

What about money? It is comprised of paper bills and metal coins. It's a medium of exchange that is more convenient and efficient than the old barter system. If I need to buy clothing, I would much rather be able to carry in my wallet the means of purchase than having to lug around a wheel barrow full of crops to trade for it. The actual substance money is comprised of is worth very little. But since everyone recognizes it to have a certain value, it does.

This much we understand about money. But yet it means so much more than this. We give it meaning. Like the flag or a placebo, money carries with it all sorts of beliefs, hopes, and expectations.

And yet, it is difficult to identify and understand the nature of these beliefs. It is far from obvious what meaning each of us attribute to money. This is due to the fact that the vast majority of our thinking is subconscious. Research indicates that more than 90% of all of our thinking is subconscious – so it is hard to even recognize the ways in which our beliefs and expectations manifest themselves.

Nonetheless, it is possible to unpack and really understand our deepest beliefs, thoughts, and expectations around money. How do we do this? By figuring out what stories we tell ourselves and ultimately believe to be true.

Publisher and television producer Lisa Cron put it this way:[7]

> *"We think in story. It's hard wired in our brain. It's how we make strategic sense of the otherwise overwhelming world around us. Simply put, our brain constantly seeks meaning from all the input thrown at it, yanks out what's important for our survival on a need-to-know basis, and tells us a story about it, based on what it knows about our past experience with it, how we feel about it, and how it might affect us."*

We all have stories we believe which form the basis of how we live our lives. Some of these stories lead to results that are self-destructive, while others are life affirming. Only by entering in to the right story can we begin to change the course of our lives for the better. As author and educator Jim Trelease explains:

"Story is the vehicle we use to make sense of our lives in a world that often defies logic."

We each have stories about money that profoundly affect our lives in countless ways. So, to understand these entrenched thoughts and beliefs about money, we have to understand our stories. These stories dictate how we live and what we ultimately believe.

In the remainder of this section, we will focus on three central questions. The answers to these questions form the basis of our money stories which drive our thought processes and behaviors.

The three questions we will explore are:

1) What is Wealth? (How is it derived? Is it a finite resource?)

2) What is Work? (How do we view work? What is the purpose of work?)

3) What is Retirement? (How do we define retirement? How do we envision retirement?)

[2]

The Nature of Wealth

Robert Malthus was a pioneer of Classical Economic Theory. He is most well-known for his theory of population and income. In 1798, he published his *Essay in the Principle of Population* which proposed an inverse relationship between population size and economic growth.

Malthus introduced the first and perhaps most famous of all demographic forecasts, ultimately concluding that population growth would outstrip available food in the 19th Century.

He derived his findings from the law of diminishing returns, which led him to believe that more people results in fewer goods for each person. Therefore, as population grows, poverty inevitably increases. According to Malthus, this was true for several reasons. First, a given amount of resources means that population growth directly impacts consumption. Second, a fixed amount of capital also means that the average production per worker will decline as the size of the labor force grows. Third, with a fixed income, there is a dilution of capital. More consumers divide a given amount of goods, and each worker receives less because there is less capital per worker.

Malthus was a well-reasoned researcher who based his theory on careful historical observations and sound logic. He also happened to be completely wrong. History unfolded in pretty much the opposite manner of what Malthus predicted. As populations grew substantially across the world, so too did food production and economies.

Why? Where did Malthus go wrong?

He started with a presupposition about the fundamental nature of wealth that was not true. He was operating under the basic premise that wealth consists of what exists. In other words, wealth is fixed and based on the amount of scarce resources throughout the world. Wealth resides in land and what is derived from it. Malthus – like all of us – had a story about money that he believed deeply. The problem was that his story was not true and that ultimately invalidated all of the work that he had done.

Malthus' experience is instructive because it reveals a financial mindset that is still extremely common to many of us. Namely, it is the idea of scarcity.

Why should we care about this? Harvard Business School's Michael Porter puts it this way:[8]

> *"What people believe about what it takes to be prosperous has much to do with how they behave."*

Our money-related decision making and behavior have everything to do with the stories we tell ourselves about where wealth comes from.

So, what did Malthus believe about that source and nature of wealth? Where did he go wrong? It turns out that Malthus was missing one crucial component: Human Capital.

Human capital is the stock of competences, knowledge, and personality attributes embodied in the ability to perform labor and produce economic value. As Churchill correctly pointed out more than sixty years ago, the empires of the future are the empires of the mind.

Since the time that Malthus unveiled his theory of population growth, worldwide per capita GDP has grown nearly twenty fold. See the chart below for a look at historical world GDP growth.[9]

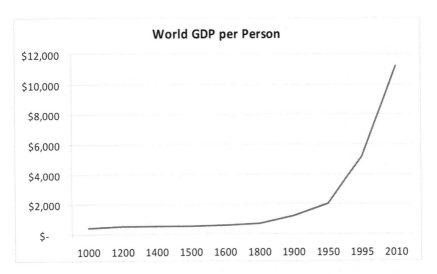

So how is it that the world is twenty times wealthier than it was a couple hundred years ago when the underlying quantity of the world's raw materials has not changed? The primary source of wealth has changed. Prior to the 1900's, physical resources were the primary source of wealth. Today, the ideas and formulas to manipulate and rearrange raw materials are the engine of wealth creation. As Stanford economist Paul Romer says, big advances in standard of living always come from "better recipes, not just more cooking."

The late Harvard economist, Joseph Schumpeter, coined the phrase "creative destruction" to describe how the engine of the U.S. economy works. In Schumpeter's analysis, the economy advances due to disruptive innovations. Such innovations create new jobs, skills, and ideas but they also render obsolete old skills, technologies, and equipment. Most significant is the net result of this process of creative destruction; It ultimately lifts the standard of living within the economy as a whole.

Perhaps the best example of creative destruction was the advent of the automobile as the preferred means of transportation. This innovation brought about a great deal of destruction for various livelihoods such as buggy whip manufacturers, stable boys, and blacksmiths. Yet, it created many more new jobs and a whole slew of related industries were created (i.e., engineers, mechanics, gas stations, auto workers).

Those who have studied the economics of prosperity around the globe have observed two basic philosophies and have determined these underlying beliefs to be the basic difference between the developed world and those parts of the world resistant to development.

These two basic philosophies revolve around the central question: What is wealth? And, consequentially, what is the basis for prosperity?

1) Wealth consists of what exists. In other words, wealth is fixed and is based on the amount of scarce resources throughout the world. Wealth resides in land and what is derived from it. This is what Malthus believed.

2) Wealth above all consists of what does not yet exist. According to this viewpoint, the potential for wealth and prosperity is limitless because it is based on ideas and insights. Wealth primarily resides in the promising processes of innovation. This takes into account the concept of human capital.

We'll call the first philosophy the scarcity mentality and the second one will be referred to as the abundance mentality. As we mentioned, all of us have many stories about money that we tell ourselves. And this one – the fundamental basis of prosperity and nature of wealth – is one that effects all of us even if never explicitly articulated.

The scarcity mentality presumes there is not enough to go around. You need to hold on, to hoard in order to protect yourself. Scarcity necessitates a dog-eat-dog world mentality. More is better. And, in general, it is going to be characterized by competition and thrift rather than collaboration and generosity.

The abundance mentality, on the other hand, is focused on "what could be" specifically as it relates to human potential. Aristotle discovered thousands of years ago that what you can do with resources increases exponentially when you focus on their potential rather than just the existing attributes of those resources.

Every single one of us is uniquely gifted. We can contribute significantly to our own well-being and in some way to the greater well-being of the world. It is simply by lack of initiative or understanding that we fail to do so. Unfortunately, as Henry David Thoreau observed:[10]

"The mass of men lead lives of quiet desperation."

We'll use the symbol of a "seed" to represent human potential and ingenuity. Despite appearances to the contrary, seeds are alive. They contain an embryo which will develop into a seedling under the right conditions. Seeds use small amounts of stored energy, staying alive and essentially "waiting" for the right conditions to begin to grow.

Likewise, human potential is essentially stored energy that is "alive" and "waiting" to emerge under the right conditions. However, also like seeds, human potential can easily die if the right fundamental conditions are not met.

We need to embrace the abundance mentality of wealth and prosperity. Wealth lies primarily in innovation and creativity and human ingenuity. We need to believe this not because it will inspire us (although it will). We need to believe this because it is true.

Research economist, William J. Baumol, has documented the rise of per capita income in conjunction with the inception of free market economies.[11] According to Baumol's research, there was a 1500 year period – from the time of ancient Rome until the start of the Industrial

Revolution – when growth in productivity and per-capita income in Europe was essentially zero.

That began to change by the 18th century when per-capital incomes in Europe increased by 20-30 percent; followed by a 200-300 percent rise in the 19th century. By the 20th century, capitalist economies grew by 700-800 percent, according to conservative estimates.

The point is this: A great number of us are living within a story that no longer exists. We are living in a world of scarcity and a zero sum game regarding wealth. Thanks to the abundance of human ingenuity and innovation unleashed within free market economies of the developed world, wealth has been created at an astounding rate and has moved far beyond being an unchanging statistic.

Look again at the GDP per capita chart. What is that showing?

It shows that there are plenty of opportunities to go around. We can share in and celebrate the success of others rather than being threatened by it. Instead of seeing life as one finite pie wherein I must maximize my own share or lose it to someone else, we should see the reality of a growing pie. It can allow us to be genuinely happy for the success of other people.

Such an understanding of the nature of wealth creation causes us to think in terms of possibility and potential rather than limitation and competition.*

All of these numbers reflect average per-capita income and say nothing about income or wealth disparities or inequalities. It does not speak to the dearth of opportunities for those lacking access to quality education, sufficient nutrition, healthcare, or family support. These are very real problems that are a "Social Capital" type of issue that will be indirectly addressed in the fourth section of this book.

[3]

The Intangible Asset

Properly understanding the nature of wealth creation and the importance of human capital *as a concept* is important, but such an understanding must become more concrete in order to have any real impact on our lives.

And in case you're tempted to dismiss this concept of human capital as too "squishy" of a subject to ever measure or substantiate, I'd point to a recent World Bank study titled "The Changing Wealth of Nations." In it, there is extensive research revealing that, on average, all of a country's natural and produced capital adds up to less than 20% of its total wealth.[12] The remaining 80% is intangible wealth, defined in the study as "human capital, social, and institutional capital." And, of these, the heaviest weighting of a country's intangible wealth is its human capital.

Now, assuming human capital consists of a person's education, skills, and abilities, we need to ask how these intangibles are most effectively leveraged and realized in economic terms. In other words, how is the vast potential of human capital actually realized? That occurs when a person is most properly engaged and utilized in the workforce.

Which leads us to our next major question: What is Work? This is a fundamental component of everyone's money stories. Just like our first question regarding the nature of wealth, it is impossible to not be guided by some fundamental story about the nature of work: What is the purpose of work? Why is it important? There are two fundamentally different answers to this question:

1) Work is primarily about the compensation received for doing it. We work in order to make a living. Work is a means to an ends to gain success or power or recognition. Work is a chore that we undertake in order to do the things that we really want to do.

2) Work is primarily about the nature of the work itself. Work is the natural exercise and manifestation of human abilities and is a means to find fulfillment. We look upon what we create through our work and find satisfaction in it.

Every single one of us fundamentally believes one of these two stories. Now, you may correctly say there is truth in both, but none of us can get off that easily. One of the two is a dominant theme for each of us and subsequently shapes our thought process in significant ways.

Several years ago, the Principal Financial Group ran an advertisement showing an athletic woman in her sixties wearing a wet suit, carrying a surfboard, and delightedly heading to the shore. The question was posed "Why do we work?" and then subsequently answered, "For the freedom that a secure retirement brings." It ended by stating, "We understand what you're working for." It is clear in this ad, and many like it, that "you" are clearly not working for the sake of the work itself. You are working toward liberation from work.

The theoretical question regarding the purpose of work forces some more practical questions: Do doctors practice medicine primarily in order to make a living or to relieve suffering? Do lawyers take on cases because it is the profession that enables them to live or because of their passion for justice?

But does it even matter *why* we do the work we do?

To answer this question, we'll look at the business world. What makes certain companies so successful? It's more than having a motivated, passionate employee base. It's also more than just trying to make a lot of money. The best companies in the world are the ones that have put purpose before profit. They have a grand vision of making the world - or some little corner of it - somehow better off. The employees of these companies are doing work that matters to them.

In *Built to Last,* Jim Collins and Jerry Porras showed that organizations driven by purpose and values outperformed the general market 15:1.[13] Another book called *Firms of Endearment* identifies thirty companies that are driven by a clear sense of purpose and that put their employees and customers ahead of the needs of shareholders. The stocks of these purpose-driven firms have outperformed their more conventional competitors by a ratio of 8-to-1.[14]

The outperforming ones are the ones steered by their purpose above all else and are much less influenced by the movement in their stock price. Ironically, it is those firms that are almost exclusively transfixed on profit and shareholders that continually underperform.

Jim Stengel, the former global marketing officer of Proctor and Gamble, said:[15]

> *"The power of purpose is not a marketing idea or a sales idea. It's a company idea. Purpose drives an entire organization and it answers why the brand exists."*

Southwest Airlines is by far the most successful company in the airline industry. Herb Kelleher founded Southwest 40 years ago. At the time the company was founded, there were immensely high cost structures associated with air travel. As a result, only 15% of the American public had ever flown at that time, since no one but the upper class could afford to fly.

So, Kelleher started Southwest with a very basic but powerful purpose. He wanted to "democratize the skies" by giving people "the freedom to fly." It is no coincidence that, since the time Southwest airlines was founded; the percentage of Americans who have flown has grown from 15% to over 85%.

In order to achieve the purpose of his company, Kelleher has maintained a laser-like focus to drastically reduce the price of flying. In order to do that, his company had to completely rethink the prevailing economic model of the airline industry. Among other ideas, Southwest established a point-to-point system rather than the less efficient "hub and spoke" model.

The key part of the story of successful companies is the effect that purpose has on the employees. In his book, *It's Not What You Sell*, Roy Spence states:[16]

> *"Purpose turns employees into evangelists, which turns strangers into customers, and customers into fans. It's absolutely contagious."*

You can see this sort of corporate "evangelism" from employees at firms such as Whole Foods, John Deere, and BMW. Each of these companies has a focused sense of purpose that has rallied the workforce and turned them into advocates.

That same sense of purpose that has guided the world's most successful companies and inspired their employees can and should guide each of us as we navigate our daily lives.

Too many people go through life without much enthusiasm or a sense of excitement. Frequently this is due to the fact that they are doing or being something or someone who they are not. It is incongruent, and it often leads to depression, burnout, or just being ineffective. That's why it is important to gain a much better understanding of what is truly important to you and develop a strong sense of purpose around that theme.

Roy Spence says it this way:[17]

> *"If you have a purpose and can articulate it with clarity and passion, then everything makes sense and everything flows. You feel good about what you're doing and clear about how to get there. You're excited to get up in the morning and you sleep easier at night."*

In other words, our work *matters*. In the aforementioned examples, the functional reason employees of these firms do the job they do is because it helps other people.

As Dorothy Sayers articulated 70 years ago:[18]

> *"Work is not, primarily, a thing one does to live, but the thing one lives to do."*

[4]

The Right Kind of Work

In his ground-breaking book *Flow,* Mihaly Csikszentmihalyi explains what his research showed to be human beings' primary source of happiness: work. Not just any work, but rather what he deems to be "optimal experience" or "flow." He calls it that because many of the respondents in his research described the feeling as an almost automatic, effortless, yet highly focused state of consciousness. What his research ultimately reveals is a high correlation between concentration and happiness.[19]

People are at their happiest when they are completely immersed in a project or task. So if through our work, we can ultimately express our unique gifts to the world around us and obtain our greatest individual happiness, then we need to better understand and redefine exactly what is meant by work in this context.

Extrapolating a bit on Csikszentmihalyi's research, we are ultimately designed to make a unique contribution to the world around us. And one of the best ways to do that is to figure out our unique strengths/gifts/talents and capitalize fully on them. Once we start to understand what it is that we are both good at and enjoy doing, then we should do more and more of it. We should get "lost" in those activities and make a positive contribution in the process.

There are a number of great tools to determine your strengths. One that I'd recommend is the StrengthsFinder tests developed by the Gallup organization. They have an abundance of research that has gone into their testing and also some great ideas for practical application.

The StrengthsFinder tests categorize 34 different talent "themes" into four broader domains:

1) *Strategic Thinking* – These are the people that keep us all focused on what we could be. They continually stretch our thinking for the future by constantly absorbing and analyzing information.

2) *Relationship Building* – People with strength in this area are the essential glue that holds a group together. They can create groups or organizations that are much greater than the sum of their parts.

3) *Influencing* – Those with strength here are always selling ideas to people inside or outside an organization. They can help an idea reach a much broader audience.

4) *Executing* – People who know how to make things happen. When you need someone to implement a solution, these are the people who will work to get it done. Those with this strength can "catch" an idea and make it a reality.

Either in lieu of or in addition to taking a test such as StrengthsFinder, there are also a few questions on the next page that can help you identify unique talents.

- What are the gifts you hold that have not been brought fully into this world?

- What is it about you that no one knows about?

- When you feel empty and directionless in life, what is missing in your life during those times that is causing you to feel that way?

[5]

Redefining Retirement

> *"(W)ork consists of whatever a body is obliged to do, and...play consists of whatever a body is not obliged to do... There are wealthy gentlemen in England who drive four-horse passenger-coaches twenty or thirty miles on a daily line, in the summer, because the privilege costs them considerable money; but if they were offered wages for the service that would turn it into work, then they would resign."*

– *Huckleberry Finn* by Mark Twain[20]

Our understanding of the meaning of work will inform how we understand leisure and vacation. If work is a means to an end, it is going to be something we put up with in order to enjoy our vacation time. If, on the other hand, our work is the source of great meaning and purpose for us, we will look at our rest and vacation time as a needed change in rhythm that refreshes us in order to get back to work and be able to re-engage more productively.

Many of us have a highly bifurcated outlook. We either work or play. Many people work in order to play. We put in long days on the job with no particular goal in mind except to finish it as quickly as possible so we can relax. As a consequence, we wish our days, weeks, years, and lives away. William Butler Yeats wrote that for many people:

"Life is a long preparation for something that never happens."

As a financial planner, the task of interpreting a client's goal is not just part of the job but the main part. A person's definition of a goal is inseparable from the means by which to achieve that goal.

So, for instance, if one of your goals is to retire at age 60, I could not help you actually achieve that goal unless I know what "retirement" means to you. In Section III, we will discuss in detail how to actually plan for retirement and how to implement the various components of a successful retirement plan. But before we do that, we need to properly define what retirement means – or should mean – to each of us.

Retirement is the lynchpin of financial planning. It is the foundational work upon which all other planning tends to rest. Therefore, how we define retirement is crucial to actually achieving that goal and also crucial in order to truly find Deep Wealth. It is also, of course, a vital component of our money stories.

Therefore, the third big question we will explore here is: What is retirement? What does it really mean to retire? How should we think about this term? Again, there are essentially two possibilities:

1) To retire means to withdraw from office or business or active work life, usually because of age. It is a time of life to relax and partake in leisure and travel. This is a standard definition of the term. Retirement is synonymous with retreat and withdrawal.

2) To retire is to become financially independent. It means you work because you want to; not because you have to. Life after retirement may look a lot like life before retirement but the key

is an internal freedom that stems from not being financially dependent on employment.

First of all, we should recognize that the first definition is by far the most common understanding of the term. It is what the vast majority of people mean when they mention the word retirement. It is also a completely antiquated notion – and a potentially harmful one – in my opinion.

The word "retirement" was popularized in the United States in the 1930's when Roosevelt was instituting the Social Security system. The retirement age for Social Security benefits was 65 and, at that time, the average life expectancy was 62. So, if you were in the fortunate minority that lived to see retirement, it was typically a very short period of time.

Think of how different it is today. A 65 year-old couple has about a 50% chance that at least one of them will live to age 90. Now, with quite a number of people retiring before 65, it is certainly reasonable to plan on 30-40 years in retirement.

But even aside from the big changes in life expectancy over the last 80 years, there is good reason to believe we've outgrown the term. One hundred years ago, the average worker was engaged in manual labor, often in factories or manufacturing plants. Workers functioned like machinery and, as such, a 65 year old could not compete with the productivity of a 25 year old.

That's what the author Stephen R. Covey meant when he said:[21]

> *"To me, the whole concept of retirement is a flawed notion, a culturally misaligned relic of the Industrial Age."*

Mitch Anthony, author of *The New Retirementality*, put it this way:[22]

"We have been hanging onto that concept, but it no longer makes sense because most of us no longer trade our physical capacity for a paycheck. We trade our intellectual capacity and our relational capacity for a paycheck."

In his book, *Encore*, Marc Freedman argues persuasively that we should consider restructuring our life cycles to essentially take more time off earlier when we need it more. He explains it this way:[23]

"Why is it that we load down individuals in their twenties, thirties, and forties with the expectation that they are most productive at precisely the juncture when we also ask them to raise children and climb up the income curve, while we essentially prod individuals from their fifties onward to stop working, or at the very least to please move out of the way?"

"Instead, why not refocus our public policies and other investments to better support young families and the frail elderly, while simultaneously expanding opportunities for those who want to continue contributing in significant ways?"

But, for the sake of argument, let's put aside this idea that we've outgrown the traditional understanding of the word retirement. Let's assume retirement is a God-given right, as so many millions seem to believe.

We still have a major problem. The mere notion of retirement in the traditional sense of the word is nonsensical based on the definition of work that we just discussed. Essentially, work is an activity that brings happiness and meaning to us individually and provides value to others. We are each designed to do some kind of work based on our unique skills and abilities. At what age would we want to stop doing that?

Blaise Pascal in his Pensees declared,[24]

"Nothing is so intolerable...as being fully at rest, without a passion, without business, without entertainment, without care"

The traditional notion of retirement means to withdraw and that's a poor premise for entering the latter phase of life. It's a negative emotion, and no creative thought develops out of a negative impulse. Yet, that is exactly what the first definition of retirement is all about: what life is not like. It does not provide a positive vision.

What we need to do is redefine for ourselves what retirement really means, much like we have redefined what wealth means and what work means. It's about asking what I am going to <u>retire to</u> rather than <u>retire from</u>. What we're now talking about is a vision for this whole other phase of life rather than a short rest period in your last days. Or, as Eleanor Roosevelt once said, *"It is not more vacation we need, it is more vocation."*

Marc Freedman articulates the new approach to retirement this way:[25]

> *"Instead of phasing out they are focusing in, attempting to find more from work, not less: more flexibility, to be sure, but equally more meaning and greater impact."*

For some people, redefining retirement means launching an entirely new career. Others are using their existing skills and applying them to entirely new causes.

Regardless of the specific form it takes, the best retirement typically involves some ideal balance between work, leisure, family, and community. A successful retirement will fully engage our core strengths and passions. And it is driven by our life's purpose.

[6]

Finding Purpose

So how do we zero in on a specific purpose? To do this, I think it is best to heed Stephen Covey's advice to "begin with the end in mind."[26]

Eugene O'Kelly was the former CEO of KPMG. After being diagnosed with terminal brain cancer, he wrote an inspirational memoir to document his thoughts and insights throughout his final days. O'Kelly concluded:[27]

> *"Morbid as it sounds, my experience has taught me that we should all spend time thinking about our death, and what we want to do with our final days, insofar as it's within our control."*

Reading O'Kelly's account of his final three and half months after his diagnosis, I realized how often I take for granted my health and my time here to do things. Kelly's book was challenging because I could see myself in his shoes as he questioned and reevaluated his priorities in life as his last days drew closer. The process of thinking through our own mortality can help us to envision what an ideal "end" would look like (i.e., what would be said at my eulogy).

With this end in mind, we can get to work today figuring out how to make it happen.

Financial Planner and author George Kinder has created three hypothetical scenarios that are extremely helpful to help unpack our purpose and gain a greater sense for what really matters:[28]

1) Assume you have all the money you could ever need. What would you do? *How would you live your life? What would you do with the money? Would you change anything?*

2) Your doctor discovers that you have a rare illness. You'll feel perfectly fine, but you will die in 5 years. *What will you do in the time you have remaining to live? Will it change your life? If so, how will you change it?*

3) Your doctor tells you that you only have 24 hours to live. *What did you miss? Who did you not get to be? What did you not get to do?*

Hopefully, by this point, you've started to uncover and clarify your purpose. It's also important to articulate it, and that can be done with a personal mission statement. A personal mission statement is a declaration about the kind of life you want to lead and who you want to be. It should be purposeful, meaningful, and inspirational. You could also think of this as a single sentence written on your tombstone: "A person who..."

This is helpful so that you can begin to consistently ask yourself in various situations throughout the day, "How would I act right now - in this situation - if I were guided by my mission statement?"

[7]

The Value & Cost of Time

Ultimately, the idea of human capital forces us to consider the importance of time. Each one of us faces constant struggles to choose between time and money. Sometimes the trade-off is obvious, such as considering a promotion which will pay more but require more time at work and less time with family.

Often, though, it is more subtle. Each of us has a limited time here on earth and we dedicate a lot of that time to money concerns (getting it, spending it, worrying about it, fighting about it, fantasizing about it). The reality is that we sacrifice our lives for money, but it happens so slowly that we barely notice from day to day.

A key requirement for finding Deep Wealth is striking an appropriate balance between human capital and financial capital. That can only be done when we have really examined the value of our time. Ultimately, both our time and our money must be seen as assets that can be used to advance our purpose in this world.

For many of us, it is very common to feel like we never have enough time. We're always busy but often not in a good way. Author Henri Nouwen said it well:[29]

> *"The great paradox of our time is that many of us are busy and bored at the same time. While running from one event to the next, we wonder in our innermost selves if anything is really happening. While we can hardly keep up with our many tasks and obligations, we are not so sure that it would make any difference if we did nothing at all. While people keep pushing us in all directions, we doubt if anyone really cares. In short, while our lives are full, we are unfulfilled."*

One of the reasons we are so busy is we have too many choices. Now, obviously freedom to choose is important, but at some point it can be detrimental to our well-being. In his book, *The Paradox of Choice,* behavioral economist Barry Schwartz makes a persuasive case that we are overwhelmed by the vast array of choices in all aspects of life.[30] From cell phone carriers to health insurance plans to retirement investments to grocery shopping, we have experienced an explosion of options.

A major contributor to our time burden and our overall busyness as a culture is this significantly increased number of choices that we research, make, reevaluate, and sometimes regret. If we treat this freedom to choose as an unmitigated good, it will infringe on our time. Often without realizing it, we are making decisions between time and freedom.

Philosopher and theologian Thomas Aquinas differentiated between what he termed "first freedom" and "second freedom."[31] First freedom is a state of opportunity and potential with a plethora of choices before us. It is full of excitement and possibility, but it is also a state where relatively little actually happens. Second freedom is where we give up the limitless possibilities and focus on a select few.

First freedom is unlimited and full of potential, but it also has an unlimited ability to monopolize our time and our life. To take control, we must intentionally reduce this vast array of options to a select few. In doing so, we show respect for the value of our time – and ultimately our human capital - and create the opportunity to actually live out our purpose.

QUESTIONS to consider:

- What's standing between me and what I want/envision?

- What's my plan for overcoming each of these obstacles?

- What resources do I have that will help me deal with these obstacles?

[8]

Summary

To illustrate how our human capital is fully utilized, let's return to the metaphor of a "seed" as a representation of our potential to improve our lives and the lives of those around us.

What pre-conditions must be met in order for a seed to germinate or take root?

First, *it must be alive.* In order to achieve the initial stage of Deep Wealth, there must be a sustaining vision of having something unique and useful to give to the surrounding world. Recognizing and believing in some particular purpose to serve is a prerequisite. We must resist the temptation to compartmentalize life by refusing to separate career related values from what we value about family, friendships, spirituality, and so on.

Purpose and unique abilities are like threads interwoven throughout a person's life and are what provides strength and passion. To identify them, we should look for recurring themes in our lives. What lessons or ideas seem to continually surface in your life? Do you see a problem that plays out over and over again and continues to pull you back to deal with it?

"Do not do what someone else could do as well as you. Do not say, do not write what someone else could say, could write as well as you. Care for nothing in yourself but what you feel exists nowhere else and out of yourself create, impatiently or patiently...the most irreplaceable of things." – Andre Gide

Second, if a seed is dormant, ***it must essentially be brought back to life.*** Distractions, indifference, and lack of motivation or discipline greatly increase the chance that my potential becomes inactive; that it enters a dormant stage. This stage is quite common. The best way to avoid dormancy or resuscitate ourselves from a dormant state is by forming a clear and distinct sense of purpose. A clear articulation and connection to purpose will activate our potential in a hurry.

"What man actually needs is not a tensionless state but rather the striving and struggling for some goal worthy of him. What he needs is not discharge of tension at any cost, but the call of a potential meaning waiting to be fulfilled by him." – Victor Frankl[32]

Third, the ***proper environmental conditions must exist.*** Seeds are created differently and, therefore, the requisite conditions, such as amount of water needed, vary. Likewise, we each have different gifts, abilities, and talents. These are innate and must be properly nurtured and developed.

In terms of environmental conditions, nothing is more important for the seed than the soil in which it is planted. Seeds need the proper soil to take root. Likewise, Human Capital can only begin to flourish if it is anchored solidly in beliefs and values. Therefore, we'll now turn to the topic of Spiritual Capital a.k.a. "the Soil."

Section II

SPIRITUAL CAPITAL: "The Soil"

"Everything can be taken from a man but one thing: the last of the human freedoms – to choose one's attitude in any given set of circumstances, to choose one's own way." – Victor Frankl[1]

[1]

The Story of a Cat

In 1974, Yuko Shimizu drew a picture of a cat; a female, white Japanese bobtail cat to be exact. The cat was oddly simplistic with 2 black dots for eyes, a beige dot for a nose, six whiskers, a red hair bow, and no mouth. This basic drawing – now known as Hello Kitty - has gone on to become a global marketing phenomenon, with annual sales of more than $5 billion per year.

"She has no mouth and no expression, which enables people to assign their own interpretation," explained Yo Kato, producer of the 30th anniversary Kitty Exhibition in Tokyo in 2004. In other words, the cryptic simplicity of Hello Kitty is her primary strength. Because she stands for nothing, she is waiting to be interpreted by a whole spectrum of people. Hello Kitty is, in essence, a mirror that reflects whatever desire or image an individual brings to her. She can stand for subversiveness to one person, cuteness to another, and nostalgia for still another.

The world of advertising and marketing aspires to win over the hearts of customers by creating a deep and lasting relationship. The most effective companies find a way to appeal to our deepest desires by tapping into a fundamental need to either reflect our identity or help us to construct a new identity. The successful firms combine consumer insights (big data) with the humanities (human needs).

Just like we discussed in the first section: money is much more than the paper it is printed on, the placebo more than a sugar pill, and the flag more than a piece of fabric. Likewise, certain brands come to represent deep meaning to us whether we can articulate it or not. The majority of us in the developed world are beyond needing to have our basic needs met. We are well into our wants and desires, and that is the void we try to fill. We can start to discern the precise shape of that void by analyzing how we are spending our money and what is driving those spending decisions.

[2]

Traditional Financial Planning

Financial planning has historically addressed the practical/quantitative issues:

What are your short term goals?

When do you intend to make that purchase?

How much will it cost?

Then we can put a plan together that addresses cash flow and investment decisions that are designed to meet those needs. That process is important and we'll get into that later on in the book. The problem with *just* doing that, however, is we're only addressing the "what" and the "how." As in, "what your goals are" and "how you are going to fund those goals." It is all very practical. And we need to be practical, but if we want to change at all, we need to also take it a step further – deeper – and start asking why.

For instance, let's say you have a short term goal of buying a BMW.

Why? Not why just any new car, but why a *BMW.* I contend that there are really four distinct primary motivators that will drive this type of decision.

1) The Need for Power – Image and Status that a car like that can convey; prestige; symbol of success.

2) The Need for Control – What this gets at is "security" as a driver. German engineering is reliable; it is a prudent long term investment and the best value.

3) The Need for Comfort – "The ultimate driving experience"; provides a certain freedom and experience that you do not get from just any car.

4) The Need for Approval – If you're not careful, you could confuse this with the person looking for power because image is important here as well, but you have to look closer. It's for a different reason. Rather than being most concerned about helping to shape an image that conveys authority and respect; you are more concerned with approval and the love and/or good opinion of others. This is where the "keeping up with the Joneses" idea comes into play.

Once we start to unpack this type of question, we can begin to understand our driving emotions, values, and beliefs around money. Experience and education have both led me to believe that a consistent theme will emerge for each of us. We will be looking at four different money personality types – each of which will correspond to one of the motivators above. Each of these money types will be associated with a few key characteristics which will help you to drill down to determine your primary motivator.

Once you start to see your primary money personality being revealed, you will begin to understand what's stopping you from doing what you know you need to do (whether that means saving more for retirement or getting out of debt or setting up a coherent estate plan to ultimately distribute your wealth most effectively).

As you begin to understand your primary motivation around money, you will begin to see it in nearly all your decisions and actions. I think of those dot pattern pictures that were popular in the early 90's. They were called "magic eye." If you looked at one normally, you would just see a bunch of dots in repetitive patterns. But if you relaxed your eyes and sort of refocused your vision to a deeper level, you could see a 3-D object emerge.

The same thing will happen here as it relates to your relationship with money. And that is absolutely crucial in order to have any real freedom. True financial freedom can only be realized once we begin addressing the root issues and what is beneath the surface. This is when we begin to experience Deep Wealth.

But before we even get into this topic, I want to address a common objection. It goes something like this: "Look, I really just want to focus on my finances. I'd rather not talk about spirituality or values. Just tell me what I need to do to reach my financial goals."

It's understandable that a lot of folks feel this way. The fact is we live in a world that constantly reinforces a compartmentalized approach to life. It's easy to live according to the belief that our financial lives function separately from other areas of life. But we need to realize that this is a fallacy, and a harmful one at that.

In other areas of life, we've become much more holistic. Certainly, when we think of physical health, we realize that compartmentalization does not work. If you are having lower back pain, you can go to a massage therapist and get short term relief. It may just be temporary pain; in which case a massage really is the best medicine. However, that pain could also be the sign of another issue. Pain is often a symptom of a bigger problem internally.

In the case of lower back pain, it can be a sign of chronic dehydration. Often, the pain is signaling that your body needs more water. (This pertains to a portion of the structure of the human spine which is reliant on an inner substance comprised primarily of water.) Lack of hydration can lead to pain, swelling, and even herniated disks.

Now, if I go to a massage therapist and she suggests increasing my water intake, I could tell her to just focus on my back pain: "Please don't talk to me about how much water I'm drinking – just massage the pain." It's my prerogative of course, but it is not ultimately helpful to just focus on the obvious, external issue.

My point is the interrelated nature of the body has become a widely understood and accepted concept. But this is not so with less tangible matters. That is why it is still common to hear people object to discussing spiritual or psychological matters due to the fact that they really want to focus on their financial matters as if it can all be neatly segmented and partitioned off.

What we'd all like to do is take something very complex in nature – namely, the human mind, soul, and heart – and reduce it to something much simpler. We want seven practical steps to financial success. Give me some tips I can squeeze in on a weekend that will forever change my life.

One of the major points I hope to make throughout the course of this book is that everything is connected.

Integration is desirable, but it is also unavoidable. The question is not "Is the way I handle my finances consistent with my values?" (spoiler alert: it is). But rather: "Am I aware of the connection between my financial life and my deeper held beliefs and values?"

As a financial planner, one of the most fascinating and important challenges for me has been in trying to determine the real issue of why so often financial planning is unsuccessful; why it doesn't stick. Even when people know – in crystal clear terms – what they need to do, why do they so consistently fail to do it? I'm convinced it has to do with not addressing deeper issues. In terms of the garden analogy, most of us would prefer to trim around the edges (solve immediate problems) than inspect, evaluate, and test the soil (address deeper issues).

For example, you may have a problem spending too much money, so you cut back your spending to save more. This might work for a few months, but generally the spending issues will creep back up and the same old problem will resurface. Why? Because you're effectively trimming the lawn (temporarily correcting the overspending), but not dealing with the root system beneath the surface (emptiness, broken relationship, etc).

The fact is that in many cases we have learned to search for external solutions to signals from our mind, heart, or soul that something is out of balance. From an early age, we program ourselves to look for external possessions to meet an inner need. One of my daughters cries out for her puppy blanket whenever she gets hurt or is feeling sick. She has done that for years now. Her weepy cry for "puppy" is a signal that all is not well. Puppy helps her cope, but it is not the solution.

Of course, we can see that to be true in little children. It's amusing, and yet I stop laughing as soon as I realize that I do the same thing. I have my own puppy. At times, it has been my career. At other times, it's been a relationship. These are not bad things. But at those times when they've become too central to me, there's a bigger problem I am not addressing. There is something deeper going on that needs to be understood and addressed if there is to be any hope for real change. It's a spiritual issue.

[3]

Defining Spiritual Capital

I will define spiritual capital as the degree of ability to disconnect one's attitude from one's circumstances. Gandhi is a classic example of a historical figure with immense spiritual capital. He was able to draw from a tremendous inner peace in the midst of all sorts of suffering. It was his spiritual capital that sustained him and facilitated his ability to initiate a model of civil disobedience that changed history for the people of India.

Another example is the Apostle Paul who wrote several books of the New Testament from a prison cell. He wrote some of the most inspiring and joy-filled passages in all of historical literature while confined to dreadful conditions, expecting that he was to be executed.

"Peace which surpasses all understanding"[2] would be a way to identify spiritual capital. It's not just about inner peace, but that is certainly a way in which it is commonly manifested. A person with no spiritual capital, on the other hand, would be completely at the whim of his/her circumstances.

Now, if we are honest, most of us do not have a vast resource of spiritual capital. The fact is that we are very much affected by our circumstances. If I am shunned or slighted by someone I respect, I will be hurt and perhaps even doubt my own worth in some way. The effect on the psyche can become much worse as the level of severity increases. For instance, if the people to whom I am closest - say my wife or children - reject me or disown me, I could be absolutely devastated.

These are only a few ways in which the presence or absence of spiritual capital can affect us. This same concept actually has crucial ramifications for how we perceive money and its role in our lives. The fact is we will not fundamentally change our behavior unless we first really understand why we do what we do. By exploring this idea of spiritual capital, we will begin to understand the "why" behind all of our financial decisions.

So, here is a book about money...specifically about how you manage your money and plan for your financial future that will talk a lot about spirituality and values. Not in general, but specific to you. What is your underlying belief system and how well do you understand it? How does that set of beliefs or worldview impact the decisions you make around money?

So the operative question is: How, on a personal level, do you begin to understand the "why" behind your financial decision-making?

We will do this by introducing four different money personality types and then working through each of them to understand the characteristics and implications of each.

[4]

Money Personality Types

First, a little explanation about the money personality types to be introduced here. They are fundamentally different than most others. Typically, money personality assessments focus on gauging external characteristics. For instance, one might represent a saver type, while another might represent a spender type, yet another may be a giver or a worrier.

This is different. It is less concerned with external attributes and more concerned with what's going on beneath the surface. What is the spiritual underpinning of a person's money personality type? What are the deep longings each of us is looking for money to provide? What are the driving emotions behind financial decision-making?

As I had mentioned, there are four different money types here. The first thing you'll want to do is identify which of these four best represents you. On the next page is a grid that helps you initially gauge that.

Try to select the most accurate word/description in each of the four columns to the right of the "money type" column. Then determine which one of the four money types most closely mirrors your own answers. This will give you some idea as to your money personality type, but there is also a 20 question assessment in the Appendix (see page 203) that will provide a more accurate answer as to which money type you most closely align.

Once you have completed that assessment and read the rest of this section, you will begin to better understand some of the "triggers" to look for that will symbolize potential imbalances and looming problems specific to your money type.

Money Personality Type:	The Pleasure Seeker	The Mogul	The Guardian	The Star
Worst Nightmare/Biggest Worry:	• Stress/Demands	• Humiliation	• Uncertainty	• Rejection
Positive Attribute (Strength):	• Restful/Content	• Innovative/ Decisive	• Responsible/ Self-Sufficient	• Compassionate/ Empathetic
Problem Emotion:	• Boredom	• Anger	• Worry	• Cowardice
People Around You Often Feel:	• Neglected	• Used	• Condemned	• Smothered

It is said that good gardeners do not grow plants, they grow soil. This highlights the absolutely essential role that soil plays. It is easy to forget or not realize that soil is a living thing. It is a colony of plant roots, fungi, and microscopic life that produces nutrients, fights off disease, and decomposes dead leaves and roots. Soil provides plant roots with water, food, and oxygen essential for growth. It is the source of life for the plant.

Our "soil" is our source of life – it is that combination of emotions, values, and essential character that drive us. What the four money types represent are essentially four different types of soil. Understanding the characteristics of your "soil type" will help you better understand your relationship with your money from a core level.

So, assuming you now have an educated guess as to your primary money type (your soil) – how do you begin to understand how it practically affects your decision-making around money and everything else?

I think real life, biographical examples make for the most understandable and interesting way to learn about each of the primary money motivators. So, what follows are historical examples – brief biographical sketches of famous people that fall into each of the four primary money types. Each money personality (or type of soil) has its own primary motivator (or root system). Likewise, each primary motivator gives its own meaning to money.

The chart below lays out how each of these is related. We'll go through examples of each money type so that you can begin to see, practically, how each money personality plays out in real life.

Money Personality (Type of Soil)	Primary Motivator (Driving Emotion)	Meaning of Money (Ultimate Aspiration)
The Pleasure Seeker	Comfort	Freedom
The Mogul	Power	Image/Status
The Guardian	Control	Security
The Star	Approval	Love/Self-Worth

[5]

The Pleasure Seeker: Marlon Brando

Marlon Brando is an enigma. He is widely considered one of the greatest – if not the greatest – actor of all time. And yet, he has made countless disparaging remarks about actors and the acting profession.

Here was an immensely gifted actor. And he was respected by his peers, honored with awards, and adored by millions of fans. He was an iconic presence both at the beginning of his career in the early – mid 50's (think *The Wild One*) as well as mid-career as Mafioso boss in *The Godfather.*

He spawned a huge following of imitators and emulators of his general attitude and method acting techniques. For instance, James Dean modeled his acting and his own lifestyle after his hero Brando. A young Paul Newman was greatly influenced by him and Jack Nicholson acknowledged in 1972 that "we are all Brando's children" and that "he gave us our freedom (as young actors)."[3]

Film critic Roger Ebert praised Brando as "the Greatest Actor in the World." Russell Crowe wrote and sang a song about him called "I Wanna Be Marlon Brando."

But after hitting the pinnacle of his career following *The Godfather* and the *Last Tango in Paris*, Brando essentially decided to stop acting. He would then only agree to small roles as he extracted the most money for the least amount of work in all roles he would do going forward. Ironically, it was Brando – one of the greatest actors of all time – who declared "acting is an empty and useless profession."[4]

As he got older, he refused to memorize his lines and found creative ways to keep cue cards in appropriate lines of sight. For example, his lines were written on Kal-El's diaper in *Superman* (1978).

As Rod Steiger once said, Brando had it all, great stardom and a great talent. He could have taken his audience on a trip to the moguls... But he simply would not. When James Mason' was asked in 1971 who was the best American actor, he had replied that since Brando had let his career go belly-up, it had to be George C. Scott, by default. Charleton Heston acknowledged Brando to be the greatest actor of his generation, but believed his attitude held him back considerably.

In an attempt to get a further glimpse into the psyche of the mysterious Brando, let's consider a few details of his personal biography.

Brando became obese later in life, but well before that his eating habits were already legendary. Karl Malden claimed that, during the shooting of One-Eyed Jacks (1961), Brando would have "two steaks, potatoes, two apple pies a la mode and a quart of milk" for dinner.[5] He loved ice cream and was often reported to have eaten five gallon tubs all by himself. Brando explained it by saying,

> *"Food has always been my friend. When I wanted to feel better or had a crisis in my life, I opened the icebox."*

On the topic of marriage and procreation, Brando contended,[6]

> *"I don't think it's the nature of any man to be monogamous. Men are propelled by genetically ordained impulses over which they have no control to distribute their seed."*

Brando had three ex-wives and nine children from different marriages as proof of this uncontrollable biological state.

Both indulgence and apathy are themes that we see emerge from this brief sketch of Brando's life. But what was driving him? I would suggest that it was a constant desire for freedom. The problem though is in how we define freedom. A great distinction should be made between "freedom from" doing things (negative liberty) and "freedom to" do things (positive liberty).

The idea of "positive liberty" meshes with the premier symbol of independence in the U.S., the Statue of Liberty. It represents freedom to practice religion, speak freely, pursue individual dreams, and on.

Negative liberty, on the other hand, is a freedom from any real sense of responsibility. This, I believe, perfectly encapsulates the core behind Brando's persona. Whether it was freedom from committing to marriage or maintaining a healthy diet or memorizing his lines, Brando may be best characterized by his continual rebellious search for freedom.

Brando's rebel without a cause persona both on the big screen and in real life was probably best summed up in a line from one of his iconic early performances. Playing renegade biker Johnny in *The Wild One*, he is asked, "What are you rebelling against?" Johnny replies, "What do ya got?"[7]

The Pleasure Seeker is in search of comfort and a certain type of experience above all else. For the Pleasure Seeker, money provides freedom. Ironically, those who have gotten their wish and accumulated vast financial resources have often found themselves living in a virtual prison. An endless array of possibilities and choices can be paralyzing.

Many rich people have explained how they have felt imprisoned by their wealth. This is quite opposite of how most people view the rich.

As Jessie H. O'Neill puts it:[8]

> *"prison walls can be constructed of infinite possibilities as well as a severe limitation of choices."*

[6]

The Mogul: Donald Trump

In case you've been hiding under a rock somewhere for the last twenty years, Donald Trump is a famous real estate developer turned celebrity TV personality. He so often says things that are over the top and offensive that it's hard to know where to begin. I don't know that anyone so perfectly personifies the personality type known as "The Mogul" as does The Donald. And yet, there is a certain danger in using such a larger-than-life figure because it can become more of a distraction rather than a helpful psychological profile.

So, let's forget about Trump for a minute, and focus instead more generally on a business person who "loves money" or "loves power." While the person "loves" these things, we generally would not think of him as a loving person. The reason for this lies in the fact that the man's hunger for success, conquest, or riches is an end in and of itself. As a result, people along the way are often treated as a means to achieving that end. They are used and manipulated in order to achieve desired results.

Consider Sam Walton. His wife Helen relayed conversations she had with him years ago: "I kept saying, Sam, we're making a good living. Why go out, why expand so much more? The stores are getting farther and farther away. After the seventeenth store, though, I realized there wasn't going to be any stopping it."[9]

This type of phenomenon is what the great sociologist Max Weber was referring to when he observed that in today's world "man exists for the sake of his business, instead of the reverse."[10]

Neurosis is the condition of feeling trapped in an endless pattern of emotional suffering in which obtaining the apparent object of one's desires serves only to intensify the desire itself. More recently, the term addiction has been used to describe this type of suffering. The problem with the addict and the neurotic alike is an insatiable desire. Like spraying water in the most arid desert lands, you always need more. Similar to water that seems to dissipate nearly as soon as it touches desert lands, any hopes for pleasure from the fruits of financial success often quickly evaporate for the Mogul.

This brings us back to Donald Trump. In his own words, he says:[11]

> *"My attention span is short...Instead of being content when everything is going fine, I start getting impatient and irritable. So I look for more and more deals to do. On a day in which I've got several good ones in the works and the phone calls and faxes are going back and forth and the tension is palpable – well, at those times I feel the way other people do when they're on vacation."*

If I am the Mogul, I'd rather you respect me than like me. Moguls often tend to be great leaders. They have conviction and it motivates those around them as well. Often, they are innovative and successful at branding what it is they do well. But the "shadow" side is as ominous as the aforementioned strengths are impressive. In particular, the Mogul often struggles with an over-inflated sense of self-importance. An arrogant and condescending attitude is not uncommon.

To quote The Donald:

> *"Show me someone without an ego, and I'll show you a loser."*

In *Mere Christianity*, C.S. Lewis said:[12]

> *"Pride is essentially competitive...pride gets no pleasure out of having something, only out of having more of it than the next man."*

And this sentiment gets to the heart of what is really ailing the Mogul. It's a lack of contentment. In fact, often the Mogul is so driven that even the word "contentment" is a negative by comparison. The thought of being content can conjure up ideas of laziness or lack of vision and initiative. But, that is not at all what I mean by it.

I think Nassim Taleb captured the essence of what I'm referring to when I talk about contentment. He explained the fundamental nature of what he considers to be happy people:[13]

> *"We know that people of a happy disposition tend to be of the satisfising kind with a set idea of what they want in life and an ability to stop upon gaining satisfaction. Their goals and desires do not move along with the experiences. They do not tend to experience the internal treadmill effects of constantly trying to improve on their consumption of goods by seeking higher and higher levels of sophistication. In other words they are neither avaricious nor insatiable."*

It does not take much imagination or thought to conjure up many examples of discontent. In fact, sociologists are awash in studies that show the inverse relationship between progress and happiness. In other words, the more prosperous we have become as a society, the less happy we are. A lack of contentment with what we have is the cause for a lot of the unrest and general unhappiness that abounds.

For the Mogul, there is often disenchantment with the American Dream. In many cases, the entrepreneur who is the esteemed model of success within his field of expertise is also the father and husband who left his family behind. All too often the middle-age business tycoon awakens to the realization that money not only did not solve his problems, but actually created a few more. The Mogul has believed thoroughly that life's meaning is found in obtaining maximum power and influence over others. And, consequently, money is viewed as a principle means of achieving the prerequisite status and image.

In anticipation of some readers' objections at this point, I do want to offer a clarification. Ambition in and of itself is neither a vice nor a virtue. It depends on the object and intensity of its desires. *We should aspire to be content with what we have; not with who we are.* Discontent can be healthy and is, in fact, crucial when it comes to the hard work of building character and realizing potential.

[7]

The Guardian: Howard Hughes

With personal wealth exceeding $1 billion by the 1960's, Howard Hughes was one of the richest men of his era. He had a 25 year career in Hollywood as a producer of some extremely influential and acclaimed movies such as *Hell's Angels*, *The Outlaw*, and *Scarface*.

He was also a lifelong aircraft enthusiast, pilot, and engineer. He set a number of world records with some of the aircraft he built, including setting a transcontinental speed record. His aircraft flew non-stop from LA to NYC in just under 7 hours and 30 minutes. Hughes received many awards as an aviator, including a special Congressional Gold Medal in 1939 *"... in recognition of the achievements of Howard Hughes in advancing the science of aviation and thus bringing great credit to his country throughout the world."*[14]

He went on to form Howard Hughes Medical Institute, the second largest private foundation in the United States.

Yet, despite a lifetime of astounding successes as an aviator, movie-maker, entrepreneur, and philanthropist, Hughes is best known for his bizarre reclusive behavior in the years preceding his death.

He suffered from severe obsessive-compulsive behavior. He went from being one of the most visible men in America to vanishing from the public scene altogether.

Howard Hughes would be an extreme example of the money personality known as "the Guardian." The Guardian is a type of soil that is particularly prone to having problems with the weed of control. Of course, it's not all bad. Remember, Hughes was extremely rich. Not uncommon among the guardian types, he was a great saver and accumulator of financial resources. While Hughes himself spent money in some very bizarre ways, overall he was still quite responsible in his stewardship of a huge estate. Frugality, responsibility, and prudence are typical admirable qualities of the Guardian.

So, what is wrong with that you might ask? After all, the Guardian, in many ways, is an exemplar of fine financial stewardship. The problem stems from an underlying current of worry and anxiety. In short, there is never enough money to stem the fears and concerns. To the Guardian, money provides security. That tends to make them good savers but it also means they have difficulty ever finding any real sense of peace. For the Guardian, in particular, his/her sense of well-being tends to fluctuate along with the market indices on the bottom of the television screen.

Let's consider some of the behavior of Howard Hughes again for a moment:[15]

- He once hired a man to spend months in a hotel room waiting for a phone call that never came.

- He always kept a barber on call although he only had his hair cut and nails trimmed once a year.
- He kept at least five young beautiful women in mansions equipped with cars, chauffeurs, guards, and expense accounts. And although he never visited them, he hired private detectives to make sure no one else did.

Why would anyone act like that? Well, aside from his psychological issues (which certainly helped exacerbate his issues), Hughes had an insatiable need for control. He may never even see these women – or hardly ever use the barber – or ever even get that mysterious phone call – but you just never know. "What if" is the question that haunts "The Guardian."

This brings us to the sad reality of Howard Hughes. One of the most brilliant minds and richest men of the 20th century spent a huge part of his life trying to avoid germs. For years, he laid naked in beds in hotel rooms in what he considered to be germ-free zones. He placed tissue boxes over his feet to protect them and burned his clothes if anyone ill came near him.

For the Guardian, life is all about having control or mastery over a certain area or areas of life. Having money can create the illusion of being in control of a life or destiny. The accumulation of money does not provide real security. It can actually exacerbate problems. Often, as a person's net worth increases, their isolation from culture increases as well. The resulting isolation and loneliness can create more anxiety which leads to an attempt to accumulate more control. It is a vicious cycle.

If we think about it from within the framework of the garden example, you can't "fix" a plant; you can only give it the right conditions – water, sun, and soil – and then wait. It will do the rest. The problem with organic growth is that you really can't see it. It is to some extent mysterious. And the Guardian hates the mystery of organic growth.

[8]

The Star: Andrew Carnegie

Andrew Carnegie's life has often been cited as the true "rags to riches" story. Having grown up in Pittsburgh, I've witnessed how Carnegie left his mark all over the Steel City. Even the label "steel city" owes itself largely to the life and legend of Andrew Carnegie. He made his fortune in the Steel industry, founding the Carnegie Steel Company which ultimately became US Steel. Perhaps even more noteworthy than his brilliant entrepreneur career is his astounding record of philanthropy. Estimated to be worth nearly $300 billion in today's dollars, he ultimately gave away the majority of his money to found local libraries, schools, and universities.

In the late 1800's, Carnegie wrote *The Gospel of Wealth*, in which he talked about two stages of the life of a wealthy industrialist. The first was the gathering and the accumulation of wealth. The second part, he argued, should be focused on the subsequent distribution of this wealth to charitable causes.[16] According to Carnegie, philanthropy is essential to making life worthwhile.

The successes of Carnegie both in charitable endeavors and as an entrepreneur are extremely impressive and admirable. But what really made Carnegie tick? What was it – ultimately – that drove his financial prowess and decision-making at the deepest level? To best answer these questions, we should pay close attention of some details of his personal life.

Carnegie kept a personal file labeled "Gratitude and Sweet Words" and his secretary had a daily task of cutting out favorable comments from the press and filing them away for his enjoyment.[17] He had a certain need to please that does not seem to fit with the image of a ruthless robber baron. While he may have been selective in whose opinions he valued, he certainly craved validation and approval from those people.

One key example of Carnegie's need for approval was apparent in his relationship with his long time business partner Henry Clay Frick. David Nasaw writes in his biography of Carnegie:[18]

> *"Carnegie needed more from Frick than the younger man was willing to give. Carnegie wanted Frick's loyalty and friendship; he wanted to be appreciated, respected, admired, and even loved by the younger man."*

But Frick - while happy to be Carnegie's business partner - was not interested in becoming a friend or confidant. Still, Carnegie was nearly smothering in his communications and advice to the younger Frick.

In his continuous quest for approval and appreciation, Nasaw explained how: *"Carnegie went out of his way to solicit interviews and indulge the journalists who appeared at his doorstep. He was immensely proud of all that he had accomplished and wanted the wider public on both sides of the Atlantic to share his joy."*[19]

The fact is Carnegie – recognized at the turn of the 20th century as the world's richest man – desired public admiration more than all the material riches that he had accumulated. He was extremely concerned with his legacy and how he would be known. He wanted to be known as wise, generous, benevolent, and kind.

To this end, Carnegie was in constant pursuit of ever more praise, attention, and compliments for his good deeds. More than anything he boasted of the great and important company he kept later in life. Particularly those who paid him praise were boasted of by him.

In his commentary on Andrew Carnegie, Poultney Bigelow famously quipped:[20]

> *"Never before in the history of plutocratic America had any one man purchased by mere money so much social advertising and flattery... He would have given millions to Greece had she labeled the Parthenon 'Carnegopolis.'"*

At the heart of the Star is a need for approval. Money is ultimately viewed as a source of love and self-worth. The irony for many Stars is that the more money they accumulate, the more insecure they can become. This is perhaps most obviously apparent in the mindset of an inheritor of great wealth. She is constantly wondering whether people are actually being nice to her out of sincerity. She constantly wonders, "Do people like me as a person (out of genuine love, respect, or admiration) or are they simply being nice to me because of my money?"

A quote from Madonna in *Vogue* Magazine illuminates the craving for approval:[21]

> *"Every time I accomplish something I feel like a special human being, but after a little while I feel mediocre and uninteresting again; I find I have to get past this again and again. My drive in life is from the horrible fear of being mediocre. I have to prove I'm somebody."*

This gives some insight into the psyche of The Star.

[9]

Cultivating the Soil

As is apparent at this point, we each really have to deal with the "soil" itself in order to create any real and lasting change. The best way to combat weeds and prepare to plant the seeds is to cultivate the soil. Cultivation is generally done with a hoe and a garden tiller by disturbing the soil around the roots of the weed plant. It can be effective, but it is not a one-time chore. With each rain, irrigation, or stirring of the soil, new weed growth emerges.

Cultivation can be the most effective way to kill weeds, but it also enables flourishing by allowing rain to soak in more easily and aerating the soil. So what are a few truly effective methods of spiritual cultivation?

Gratitude –

"Gratitude unlocks the fullness of life. It turns what we have into enough, and more. It turns denial into acceptance, chaos to order, confusion to clarity. It can turn a meal into a feast, a house into a home, a stranger into a friend. Gratitude makes sense of our past, brings peace for today, and creates a vision for tomorrow."

- Quote from Melody Beattie

Everyone wants to be happy. The U.S. Declaration of Independence begins under the auspice of life, liberty, and the pursuit of happiness. In one sense, happiness is completely within our grasp. Psychologists have found that it is actually emotionally and psychoanalytically impossible to be both grateful and unhappy at the same time. Gratitude fosters happiness; it's a scientifically proven fact.

But how do we cultivate gratitude?

It really has to become a habit. To foster an attitude of thankfulness in everyday life, I'd suggest starting a practice of daily giving thanks for five things that happened that day. At first, it may seem a bit hokey, but this simple practice can change the way you see the world around you. These don't have to be big things; a ray of sunlight shining through a window, a child's smile, a beautiful sunset, a cool breeze, etc.

What will happen as you begin this practice is that you will be more conscious of these types of things on a regular basis, and you will begin to live more in the moment of everyday life as you focus on these events – both big and small. Being grateful and being "in the moment" – being present – will go a long way in cultivating your soil.

Researchers have found that new habits take at least 21 days to form in the subconscious. So, I'd recommend practicing gratitude for a period of 21 consecutive days.

Contentment –

John Bogle, founder of Vanguard Mutual Funds, said it well in his book *Enough.*[22]

> *"Not knowing what is enough subverts our professional values. It makes salespersons of those who should be fiduciaries of the investments entrusted to them. It turns a system that should be built on trust into one with counting as its foundation. Worse, this confusion about enough leads us astray in our larger lives. We chase the false rabbits of success; we too often bow down at the altar of*

the transitory and finally meaningless and fail to cherish what is beyond calculation, indeed eternal."

Roman philosopher Seneca asserted:[23]

"No one can be poor who has enough, nor rich who covets more."

In the *Consolation of Philosophy*, Boethius wrote:[24]

"Nothing is miserable unless you think it so; and on the other hand, nothing brings happiness unless you are content with it."

Barry Schwartz, in his insightful book *The Paradox of Choice*, referred to "satisficers" as those people who can evaluate an array of options until they find one that is good enough and then stop looking.[25] This is a characteristic to aspire to if we are to have any hope of achieving true happiness.

Generosity –

What if contentment is actually found in the exact opposite place that we have been looking? What if contentment is found not in *accumulating* more, but rather in *giving* more? We can intellectually grasp how contentment would lead to generosity: the less we need, the more we will have to give away. But this is a trap many folks fall into by thinking that "once I have this much $ or earn this much $, then I will be able to give much more away." Of course, in most cases, that theoretical point of contentment never comes and so the intended generosity does not materialize.

But is it possible that generosity breeds contentment? There are several reasons to believe so.

- Generosity can lead to a healthy understanding of how much we already have. Giving to those in need can help a person quickly realize how much they have to give, as a different perspective and new frame of reference emerges as to how much is enough.

- Generosity can lead to a happier, more fulfilled life. Research has shown generous people to be happier, healthier, and more satisfied with life overall than those who are less generous.

- Generosity can help us value what we already own. People who volunteer their time tend to make better use of their remaining time. Likewise, people who donate money are less wasteful with the money that remains.

[10]

Feedback Loops

The link between generosity and contentment leads to one last and very important point in understanding how to cultivate spiritual capital. Our three methods of soil cultivation – Gratitude, Contentment, and Generosity - are related. But their relationship is not linear and in direct proportion to one another.

Instead, the relationship is actually representative of a feedback loop, whereby a small change creates an effect that causes an even bigger change. It's like a ball rolling down an increasingly steep hill. This is important because it means that the introduction of even small changes are then amplified and have the capacity to bring about real transformation. The nature of this change can be good or bad, depending on what type of change is introduced.

The basic essence of the relationship is as follows: 'A' produces 'B' which produces 'C' which produces more of 'A' and so on...

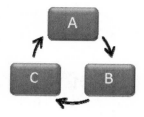

The following diagram depicts two polar opposite representations of the feedback loop. Figure 1 is the Cycle of Abundance and Figure 2 is the Cycle of Scarcity.

Figure 1: The Cycle of Abundance   Figure 2: The Cycle of Scarcity

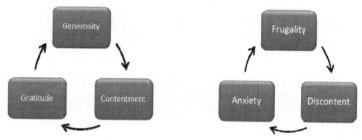

The Cycle of Abundance functions as follows:

"The more I give away, the more content I am. The more content I am, the more gratitude I feel for what I have. The more grateful I am, the more I want to give away." This cycle stems from the Abundance Mentality discussed in Section 1 where the "pie" continues to expand and there is plenty to provide for everyone.

The Cycle of Scarcity functions according to a different pattern:

"The more I keep to myself, the less content I become. The more discontentment I feel, the more anxious and concerned I become about not having enough. The more anxiety I feel, the more frugal I become." This cycle is a natural outgrowth of the Scarcity Mentality from Section I. According to Scarcity, there is a finite "pie" and everyone needs to stake a claim on his/her share.

[11]

Root Systems

Roots are the life centers of plant life. They anchor the plant in soil and take up water and minerals needed for the plants to survive and thrive. Roots can be divided into two primary categories: Primary Roots which extend vertically into the soil (these are akin to our central emotion or primary motivator) and Secondary (or Lateral) Roots which branch off horizontally from the primary root and are generally parallel with the surface.

Likewise, our "roots" are at the center of our being. This is ultimately what is held "nearest and dearest" and closest to the heart. Nearly every culture around the world uses the word "heart" to describe all that is central, core, or foundational. A person's heart is subservient to its spiritual master. For us, the "root" is the spiritual master which exerts control over the heart.

Everyone has a spiritual master. Ancient wisdom and modern psychology actually agree on this. In addressing the Ten Commandments of the Bible, Martin Luther claimed that they all flow from the first one which is that we should have no other gods. In other words, the Commandments were ordered that way for a reason, and if you break any of the other nine, it is essentially due to having some other "god." It all comes down to a heart issue and this innate human need for a spiritual master.

Existentialist philosopher Soren Kirkegaard agreed when he defined sin as putting your identity in anything other than God.[26] Fast forward to 20th century psychology. Even Sigmund Freud, who certainly did not espouse traditional religious beliefs, inferred our intrinsic need for a spiritual master of some sort. He talked about the "paralysis" that exists in the link between a person of lesser power to one of greater power. Freud went on to explain that man has "an extreme passion for authority" and "wishes to be governed by unrestricted force."[27]

Psychoanalyst Erich Fromm explained how this comes about:[28]

> *"In order to overcome his sense of inner emptiness and impotence, [man]...chooses an object onto whom he projects all his human qualities: his love, intelligence, courage, etc. By submitting to this object, he feels in touch with his own qualities; he feels strong, wise, courageous, and secure. To lose the object mean the danger of losing himself."*

So, what does this have to do with personal finance? A lot, actually. If we go back to the BMW example – what is driving that purchase? If you are a Mogul, what is really at the root of that decision? Well, first, we defined the Mogul as someone who looks to money as a source of status. The driving value/motivator is a need for power. Power is the main root that runs deep into the soil.

But plants also have secondary or lateral roots which run horizontally below the surface. These lateral roots branch off from the main root, but are absolutely crucial to the survival of the plant. This lateral root is your "god." It defines your identity.

These gods or sources of identity do not have to be other people. They can also be driving emotions or values (i.e. moralism or patriotism), roles (i.e. a prize fighter or a mother), or things (i.e. a career or a house).

Typically, these sources of identity are good things in and of themselves. Would anyone argue that having a family or a successful career are bad things? The problem occurs when an inherently good thing becomes an ultimate thing.

So, the task is to figure it out for you personally. What are your "roots"? In other words, what is your functional god(s)? What do you center your life and identity around?

You can go about determining this in a couple of ways. First, ask yourself what it is that – if taken away/if you lost it completely – would absolutely devastate you and cause you to give up your will to live. Now, this is not an indictment against deep sorrow and mourning. Certainly, there are many horrible circumstances that can justify tremendous grief. Stoicism and detachment are not the goal.

But I'm talking about a different level of response. What is it that so defines you that if you lost it, you would no longer even want to go on living? Maybe if you are a business owner, it is your business. It could be your career or your house or your role as a mother or father or significant other.

Again, these are good things in and of themselves. But if you begin to "worship" them – center your life upon them – you are not free. There is only an illusion of freedom as long as things are going well.

Another way to determine your root(s) or spiritual master(s) is to consider where your mind drifts when you are waiting at a bus stop or an airport and you have nothing to do but lose yourself in thought. Is there a common subject to which your mind wanders in those situations?

Deep Wealth means finding ultimate peace, freedom, and security. These "roots" can threaten such aspirations because they anchor you –

tie your well-being – to some circumstance. You are happy/free/peaceful IF... (the market goes up, your business does well, your marriage is good, you are promoted...) A great way to see this is to look at extreme situations.

In *Man's Search for Meaning*, Victor Frankl examined his life and the lives of those around him during his time in a concentration camp. He observed people who quite literally had everything taken from them and yet maintained their dignity, character, and an unshakeable sense of peace. An abundance of spiritual capital allowed them to transcend dire circumstances.

Spiritual capital is also extremely important on a more common level. If the root that anchors you is your career, it can act as a real burden and can actually be very costly financially. For example, if you are work in a corporate culture, can you be completely creative, free, and open to offer honest opinions if your career is at the center of your life?

It is doubtful because you are just not likely to take too much risk. Instead, you will probably exert quite a lot of time, effort, and worry around making the right political moves within the firm or ensure that you don't rock the boat or become consumed with making the right impressions on all the right people.

Consider, instead, the person who values her career but does not make it the center of her life. She is unafraid to speak out if she disagrees, changes things if necessary, and spends her time concentrating on doing the best job she can instead of losing time and energy worrying about losing her job. (This is especially true if the financial capital is also there as we will discuss in next section.)

In other words, there can be an actual, material cost to this spiritual master. Let's call it a "root tax." At work, it can result in being less productive, less creative, and less willing to take worthwhile risks.

[12]

Building Spiritual Capital

Every successful gardener knows that it starts with the right soil and strong roots. So far we've talked about roots in a mostly negative manner in order to understand the potential dangers they pose. However, roots are essential to life and, therefore are not all bad. And, in any case, they are not optional. Just as plants must have roots, we as human beings have our own types of "roots," which we cannot just eliminate.

And here is where lots of people make mistakes. They identify a problem and try to eliminate it by diverting their focus. A woman in a cycle of abusive relationships might say, "I'm done with this. I don't need a man to make me feel worthwhile. I'm going to focus on my career." And she begins to feel valued through her work. Now if she's able to break the abusive cycle this way, that's great. But, she should know that she has a new "god." Instead of a relationship, it's her career.

No one can opt out. We will "worship" something. Humans – like plants – have roots that serve as an anchor for everything going on above the surface. We all have something we form our lives around. As Bob Dylan said, "You gotta serve somebody."[29] No matter how free we think we are, in some way we all live to serve a spiritual master.

To build spiritual capital, we must first identify our root(s). As we've gone through this topic, have you begun to identify anything that you are building your life around? What is central to your identity?

Then, once you've identified the root(s), focus not on removing it but *replacing* it. (Because, again, it is certain you will have a root system; the only question is what will it be?) Strive to replace it with something that cannot be taken away. This is where God with a capital "g" comes in. And don't think you can let yourself off the hook by saying "oh, yes, I believe in God already..." Everyone has some sort of "functional savior" that rivals any professed spiritual belief. It is a continuing struggle for every one of us.

The objective here is pretty simple, really. We want peace and freedom that is not conditional. The kind that is not circumstantial. That is an integral part of what it means to have Deep Wealth. We want to be rooted in what will not and cannot be taken away. That is the paradoxical truth Jesus Christ was pointing to when he said you must lose your life to find it.

The natural tendency is for our lives to always be centered on something or someone in this world, and unless we make a conscious effort to "lose" that life, we will not truly "find" our lives in their fullest. If the default is to live in obedience out of necessity, real freedom is found by choosing to live in obedience out of love.

The fact is what we love *the most* will rule our lives. Most times the problem isn't that we love the wrong things, but that our loves are out of order. The consequences of our disordered loves are messed up lives. We love things and use people. We might say we love God, but truth be told, our hearts long after something else that we think will fill us up or make us happy.

We will unpack this more in Section IV but for now, suffice to say we want the strongest roots, the kind that are not jeopardized by negative stock market headlines or loss of a job. This is part of the essence of what it means to experience Deep Wealth.

Now we'll turn our attention from spiritual freedom to financial freedom. Now that we've gone beneath the surface to examine our deeply held thoughts and beliefs around money, we can move on to dealing with practical and effective ways to plan for and manage money.

Section III

FINANCIAL CAPITAL:
"The Green"

"I have enough money to last me the rest of my life, unless I buy something."- Jackie Mason

[1]

Positive Tension

One thing I hope has become increasingly obvious: beliefs matter. Regardless of whether we fully understand it or can articulate it, each of us has a complex web of beliefs which drives most everything we do, including the financial decisions we make. However, if we agree that beliefs matter (a lot), we should also agree that words matter. And, so, I must clarify what I mean and, more importantly, do not mean by the term "abundance."

Abundance has, in many circles, become synonymous with positive thinking or the law of attraction. That is not the case here. It is crucial to espouse an abundance mentality rather than a scarcity mentality while not falling prey to the often self-delusional and financially hazardous "think and grow rich" philosophy. In fact, much of what you will see in this section – dealing primarily with the practical components of Deep Wealth – is built around negative considerations.

An effective financial plan should always consider what can go wrong. Specifically, the goal is to construct a plan based on conservative assumptions that takes into account various contingencies that could capsize even the best of intentions. We should consider all the potential types of risk.

We need to hold in tension these two seemingly conflicting ideas:

1) An abundance mentality which believes in the limitless potential of human ingenuity to innovate and create wealth
2) A framework of critical thinking and realism that considers a world fraught with dangers and often unforeseen risks

So, from a financial perspective, should we be optimistic or pessimistic?

Yes.

To be an investor of nearly any sort you need to have a fundamental belief in the free enterprise system. We've all heard the phrase "investing for the long term." Now, that only means something if you actually believe in the long term. That is to say that you have a fundamental optimism that over time the economy will continue to grow and stocks will continue to rise.

If you are fundamentally pessimistic about the future of the U.S. economy (which is becoming more inextricably connected with the world economy), you are in a tough situation as an investor. That is particularly true if you are "The Guardian" we talked about in the last section, whereby you look to money to provide your security. If financial Armageddon is coming, you should only be investing in guns, ammo, and canned food.

The point is there is little actionable advice for the true worst case scenarios. If you are deeply pessimistic about the future of the economy and the world in particular, there is little to be gained through financial undertakings. Ultimately, money has no intrinsic value. As I mentioned in Section I, money only has value because we make it so.

We infuse it with meaning and value. If the trust that underlies our economic system deteriorates, money becomes mere paper. It is worthless. By contrast, the abundance mentality and understanding of wealth necessitates a certain sense of optimism.

But, while we are fundamentally optimistic from an investment perspective, we should be somewhat pessimistic from a financial planning perspective. Why? Because, to a large extent, the planning process involves decisions that we can make and have at least some control over the outcome.

We have options and various approaches we can choose to take. It is helpful and prudent to build a plan on a solid foundation. We should use assumptions that are pretty conservative and can withstand some tough scenarios, including death, disability, or severe market downturns.

[2]

A Puzzle

Financial planning is often illustrated as a puzzle where all the pieces fit together. And that's accurate. All of our financial decisions are interrelated. The way the investments are allocated will impact the amount of income taxes that are due which will affect cash flow needs from the portfolio which will in turn affect how much you need to save for retirement and so on...

But what is the single most important piece of a puzzle? It is the picture on the front of the box. It's easy to jump right in and begin trying to put it all together, but you'll want to understand what you're trying to build and make sure it's something that is consistent with what is ultimately most important to you. You cannot make the best financial decisions for your life until you know what the picture on the front of the box should or could look like.

You may not know what that picture looks like at this moment and so that's where it helps to begin to ask perhaps the most important planning question: "What if?"

We actually laid out forms of these "what if" scenarios in Section I to help determine your purpose. I'd suggest revisiting that section to get a better understanding of purpose and how that might relate to more practical financial concerns. What would you do differently given your understanding of your primary purpose? If you're currently employed, would you maintain the same profession or consider a career change? Would you re-evaluate your goals and how you currently prioritize your time?

The key exercise is to consider change. One of the most fundamental shortcomings in financial planning occurs when people skip over this step altogether. The easiest thing to do is to look at the current situation and project it forward, instead of stopping to consider whether you are even on the track you want to be on. Will the current path ultimately lead you to a fulfilling life?

Once we've opened our minds to new possibilities and opportunities, then we need to begin getting specific by determining goals and objectives. Goal setting is a crucial component of any successful financial plan.

There are three steps to embark on an effective goal setting process:

1) Write down your goals
2) Explain why your goals matter
3) Take the first step

Let's look briefly at each of these three.

Put it in Writing

As part of a social science experiment, two randomly chosen groups of people were asked to volunteer on an AIDS awareness program at local schools. Group A was asked for a verbal commitment to the volunteer project. Group B were asked to commit to the volunteer project as well but were also given a simple form to fill in. Of the volunteers from Group A, 17% of them actually showed up to their assigned local school. By comparison, 49% of the volunteers from Group B signed up.[1]

The takeaway is this: Writing things down improves commitment. Less than one in five of the people from the control group (A) volunteered after verbally committing to do so. The number jumped to nearly 50% simply when a written commitment was introduced.

The first key is to put your goals down in writing. Something happens in the mind when we write down our goals. There is some sort of personal accountability that is initiated when we express our goals in written form.

There are two different types of goals: quantifiable and aspirational.

Aspirational goals are important because these are what really give color to what you want life to actually look like. They are not often quantifiable by nature, but should give a fairly concrete idea of what you are hoping to do in the future. In short, what are your hopes and dreams? What does an ideal future look like for you – 2 years from now? 5 years? 10 years?

Quantifiable goals should be specific both in terms of amount and timing. The acronym for these types of goals is SMART. They should be

      Specific
      Measurable
      Attainable
      Rewarding
      Time Bound

For instance, "buying a Volvo" is not a very good goal. But buying a Volvo in two years for $45,000 cash is a well-defined goal because it provides specifics. Another example of a quantifiable goal is prefunding education costs. Education goals need to be as specific as possible. Do you want to fund all or a portion of a child's college costs? How many years and what type of school would like to plan for?

Substantiate Your Goals

In a study conducted by a group of researchers, two groups of people were asked how likely they were to vote in an upcoming election. In the first group (the control group), they were not asked anything else. In the second group, the people were asked to give a reason why they were going to vote (they could give any reason they wanted). When Election Day came, the actual voter turnout for all of those who responded "yes" to the question of whether they were going to vote was 61.5% for the first group. Turnout for the second group was 86.7%.[2]

It's important to note: The researchers only looked at the turnout of people from both groups who said they were going to vote. Yet substantially more people (86.7% vs. 61.5%) voted after they had given a reason *why* they said they were going to vote. What was the difference?

It's all about consistency. We all tend to subconsciously act with consistency to earlier decisions. If we understand this, we can use this type of behavioral tendency to our advantage.

Giving a reason for why you want to achieve each particular goal helps to form a conviction that the goal is important and worth pursuing. Once you form that conviction, it is more likely you will follow through with it. This is due to the innate impulse to behave consistently with our commitments.

Substantiating your goals provides another benefit as well. If you provide a specific rationale as to why you want to achieve each goal, you will be reinforcing the importance of that goal and providing further motivation for achieving it. In the aforementioned SMART goal framework, the 'R' stands for Rewarding. It is helpful to reflect on why the goal will be rewarding to you and/or your family. In what ways will it help? What impact will it make? Start to envision it becoming a reality.

What's important to understand here is that the real struggle is between deferred gratification and immediate gratification. Immediate gratification tends to win out because it is more compelling. We are emotional creatures who are driven to act on choices that provide the most visceral and compelling reasons. The task then is to really connect – at an emotional level – with the gratification and fulfillment to be experienced if the deferred gratification scenario comes true. In other words, if I meet my goals, how will my life be better? In what ways will I experience that?

Once we've written down our goals and substantiated why they are meaningful, we need to consider how the plan can actually come to life. Far too often, financial plans sit on shelves gathering dust and do not actually make a difference in people's lives.

Every one of us needs to admit that our internal modus operandi is to maintain the status quo and resist change of any sort. To overcome that resistance, we need to take the first step, which can best be achieved by setting up systems that automate the desired implementation.

Turn on the Sprinklers

I live in Colorado which has a pretty arid climate. Particularly in the western part of the state, there is little humidity and infrequent precipitation. In this type of environment, it's crucial to water vegetation on a regular basis; otherwise things will dry up quickly. Now, you can try to do it with a watering can or hose, but most people here use sprinkler systems for their lawns and gardens. The great thing about sprinklers is that they are automated. You do not need to worry about whether you forgot to water the lawn today or if you'll have time to get around to it. It is an automated process.

We need financial "sprinkler systems" as well. Too often, we have admirable ideas of what we're going to do, but all we have in the end are good intentions. Nice ideas with nothing to show for it. A primary differentiator between a successful financial plan and an unsuccessful one is the degree to which it is implemented. And it has been my experience that people have far more success in achieving their financial goals when they automate as much as possible.

So, whether the goal is to save an extra $1000 per month or pay off your debts or gift a certain amount to your children or church, it is best to establish automatic and recurring transfers of funds from a checking account to wherever it is going. This process is generally referred to as an "ACH" (automatic clearing house) and is the system by which financial institutions can transfer funds electronically between one another based on standing instructions from the client.

By automating savings goals, you make things happen. It is not a case of "next month I will start to do it" or needing to remember each time to write a check and hoping you have enough money in the account left over to cover it. Instead your goals are given first priority in terms of cash flow needs.

But this involves a shift in attitude as well. Instead of being passive and spontaneous we become active and intentional. The default mode for most of us is the former. Typically, at any given time, you will take action to work toward your defined financial goals if all of the following occur:

* You happen to think about it
* You have enough cash available in your account
* You have a checkbook, credit card, or other payment method on you
* You are actually motivated to do it

For most people, the probability that the stars align and all these things happen on a consistent basis is pretty low.

What *does* work is an automated process. Much like a sprinkler system providing moisture to bring about lush vegetation, automated cash flows facilitates the development of financial capital. Some examples of ways to do this are as follows:

- Automate your gifting plan – This may mean establishing a charitable trust or something simpler such as an automatic transfer out of your account every week or every month.
- Pre-fund educational goals for children and/or grandchildren – You could establish 529 college savings plan(s) and have some pre-determined amount transferred each month from your checking account into the plan(s).
- Pay off your debts – Get on an accelerated payment plan. Increase the amount that you pay every month by some amount that will amortize the debt down 5, 10, or 15 years sooner.
- Save for retirement – Once you know how much you need to save each year to reach your retirement goals (we will discuss this calculation later in this section), then automate that process on a monthly basis by having a certain amount transfer from your checking account to the appropriate investment account(s).

This is the first step in terms of implementation – automating the process of actually funding your goals through cash flow. You would then want to automate the investment instructions where appropriate. For instance, if you are adding to a retirement account (either a 401k or an IRA), it's best to have instructions on file for how to invest new contributions. The same is true for a college savings account or non-retirement investment account. Make sure there are appropriate investment instructions for each account. This avoids having a default plan whereby new additions sit in cash.

As you do this, you are becoming more active and intentional with regard to your planning and can therefore become more confident that you will reach your financial goals.

[3]

Investing to Meet Your Goals

After you've implemented an automated plan for cash flow – whether it is transferring money systematically from one account to another or saving a portion of your income on an ongoing basis – you will need a plan for what to do with that money. Your investment strategy should be closely integrated with your financial goals. Close coordination of the two creates a blueprint for success to help you meet your financial goals over the long term.

Despite the importance of setting a plan, some investors immediately focus on which stocks, bonds or other investments to buy and sell. Many times over the years, I've been asked for investment advice right at the outset of a relationship. I routinely tell clients that our team cannot give meaningful investment advice without first understanding their situation and what they are trying to achieve.

It is possible that two people with identical balance sheets could require completely different investment strategies based on the goals they are trying to achieve, anticipated amounts of inflows/outflows, and how much risk they are willing and able to assume. What is a great investment for one person may be an awful investment for someone else.

A goal-based approach to portfolio construction allows you to choose the right type of investment strategy to ensure you increase the odds of meeting your goals. The first key to constructing a customized investment portfolio is to start with the big picture. What do you own? And what do you owe? What are the characteristics of those assets and liabilities?

For instance, some individuals and families may hold a substantial portion of their wealth in illiquid assets, such as a private business or real estate. These assets are part of the investment portfolio and need to be considered in the overall risk analysis and portfolio construction process.

A business owner with the majority of her wealth residing in a closely-held business may want to be more conservative with liquid investments because of the higher level of potential downside of the large illiquid asset. But a real estate investor with a large stake in stable, income-producing properties may invest his liquid investments more aggressively to gain more upside potential.

When you start by understanding the big picture, you can develop a comprehensive wealth management strategy that is integrated and strategic. Once you understand the big picture as it pertains to your goals and your net worth, it is important to consider the topic of risk. Risk is a commonly misunderstood financial term. Risk is not volatility, which is defined as the movement of asset prices for a certain period of time. While volatility may cause risk, it does not equal risk. Risk is the chance that your actual outcome will differ from your desired outcome.

Simply put, risk is any impediment to reaching your goals. In light of what you are trying to achieve and the specifics of your current financial situation, you can determine different types of risk or the various factors that have the potential to derail your plan. One of the best ways to do this is by engaging in contingency planning to reveal the types of obstacles or risks you are most likely to encounter in trying to reach your goals.

[4]

Weeds, Mulch & Fertilizer

The various types of risk function like weeds. The primary challenge to having a lush green garden or healthy plant life is the growth of weeds. Weeds compete with plants, flowers, and grasses for all the things needed to survive. When water, sunlight, and nutrients are absorbed by weeds, it can significantly hamper the growth of desirable vegetation.

Likewise, different types of risk compete with the assets you have in a number of ways. Left unchecked, any of these risks can overtake healthy progress toward your goals. It's important to understand all the various types of risk because they work in different ways and pose numerous challenges.

Some weeds are obvious, while others are hardly noticeable. Given the intense stock market volatility we've seen in recent years, most investors are quite familiar with market risk. Other risks are less obvious, but no less insidious. For instance, inflation risk can pose a major hurdle in trying to reach your financial goals. But the threat is often less visible because its impact is less sudden. Gradually, over time, the purchasing power of your assets becomes less and less. The price of a gallon of milk or a gallon of gas is twice the amount it cost 20 years ago, but it's not a change you see from day to day.

As we mentioned, market risk is a foremost consideration for investors. How do we deal with this "weed"? We use "mulch"; Mulch is a great weed suppressant.

Mulch inhibits weed growth in two key ways. First, by thoroughly covering the soil and depriving weed seeds of the light they need to germinate, mulch prevents them from gaining a foothold in the first place. Secondly, bare dirt is the perfect place for weed seeds to land and germinate. By covering all of your bare soil with mulch, most weeds will never be able to come into contact with the soil.

So what is the "mulch" we need to apply to a goal-based investment portfolio? Bonds or low volatility alternative investments. Bonds can provide a sort of buffer which prevents market risk from really devastating a portfolio. High quality REITs (real estate investment trusts), precious metals like gold and silver, and certain hedge funds are examples of alternative investments which can also serve a mulch-like purpose. The goal here is to protect and preserve the portfolio value.

Protection and preservation of the portfolio is achieved by investing in these aforementioned types of investments which have a low correlation to stocks. In other words, if bonds and certain alternative investments perform very differently from stocks, then the overall performance of the portfolio will tend to smooth out over different market cycles (i.e., less upside during bull markets and less downside during bear markets). This is a desirable strategy in order to help preserve your capital during future downturns.

However, bonds can introduce a different type of risk to the portfolio: default risk. Default risk is the chance that a bond issuer will not make the required coupon payments or repay principal to its bondholders. One way to minimize this risk is to predominantly buy high quality bonds – those with a rating between A and AAA. The higher rating means there is a lower statistical chance of default, but it also means there is little interest paid on the bond. This is the trade-off; high quality bonds (like US Treasuries, very highly rated corporate bonds, or most general obligation municipal bonds) tend to be very reliable and stable in nearly all market conditions, but they pay less compared to other investments.

High quality bonds are like expensive mulch. There are many different types of mulch and some may not give you the "return" you are expecting. For example straw, grass clippings, or chopped leaves cost little or nothing to apply but tend to break down quickly and may not provide the protection you need from weeds. These are more like "junk bonds" which can be attractive because they are less expensive, but may ultimately fail when tested by more extreme climates or the test of time.

On the other hand, more expensive mulches tend to be much more reliable and less subject to "default." In general, bonds should primarily be purchased in order to provide stability and capital preservation and therefore should be skewed toward the high quality end of the spectrum.

The challenge in developing an appropriate portfolio management strategy is to find the right mix of investments that will generate the desired returns while at the same time controlling volatility. We addressed the latter concern. In order to control volatility or address the issue of market risk, bonds and/or certain alternative investments should be utilized.

But what about the need to generate the desired returns? Or, asked another way, do you need growth at all? Some people have enough income from Social Security, pension, dividends and interest to pay for their living expenses. Often, they will assert that they do not need to take any risk. Now, I realize this circumstance does not apply for the majority of people, but it is instructive as an example of a general principle. **Even if** you have sufficient income to cover your expenses today, you will still need to grow your portfolio. Why? Because your expenses will increase over time.

This brings us to our next "weed" that must be considered: inflation risk. Inflation has averaged approximately 3% per year over the last 80 years. That means that the cost of living doubles every 24 years. So, based on historical trends, if you have expenses of $50,000 per year today, you will need more than $100,000 in 25 years to maintain that same level of purchasing power. This means you need your investments to grow.

In order for a plant to grow and thrive, it needs a number of different chemical elements including nitrogen, phosphorus, and potassium. To make plans grow faster, they can be supplied these elements in readily available forms. That is how fertilizer works.

Stocks are fertilizer for your investment portfolio. It doesn't matter if you invest in shares of stock of a multi-billion dollar global enterprise or a tiny publicly traded retailer, when you buy shares of stock, you are purchasing a pro-rata piece of a company. The stock market is basically an auction. Investors, just like you, are making decisions with their own money in a real-time auction. If someone wants to sell their shares of a particular stock for $50 and there are no buyers at that price, the price will have to fall until someone steps in to place an order to buy.

[5]

Invest with Conviction

"The real trouble with this world is not that it is an unreasonable world, nor even that it is a reasonable one. The commonest kind of trouble is that it is nearly reasonable, but not quite. Life is not an illogicality; yet it is a trap for logicians. It looks just a little more mathematical and regular than it is; its exactitude is obvious, but its inexactitude is hidden; its wildness lies in wait."

Orthodoxy by G. K. Chesterton[3]

Prior to the financial crisis of 2008, pretty much everyone – CEOs, government regulators, Harvard MBAs, and homeowners – failed to understand the risk of a fragile financial system. Globalization creates interlocking fragility in the markets, but at the same time volatility is reduced and we therefore have the appearance of stability.

Leading business schools in the U.S. have continuously espoused and promoted an entirely analytical view of the world. Such a perspective facilitates a numerical approach where complex issues are reduced to simpler concepts. When such precision is assumed, a "black-box" approach to investing can be devised. It is tempting in so much as it allows for predictable and controllable results, but the world is too nuanced and complicated to be boiled down to equations.

When it comes to investing – especially stock investing - it's very important to know what you're buying and why you're buying it. Bernie Madoff would not have succeeded for as long as he did in perpetrating his massive fraud if investors insisted on understanding what it was they were investing in and how it worked.

Conviction is vital because it allows you to withstand severe downturns in the economy. I work with a lot of business owners and they tend to have a lot of conviction in the fortunes of their own companies regardless of the overall market environment at any particular point in time. Why? It has a lot to do with their knowledge and understanding of their single biggest asset (their business). They understand it well and believe in it.

You will likely never have quite the same level of conviction in a publicly-traded security as you would have in a business that you, yourself, founded. But you can still have a much greater level of conviction in investments that you understand well and have a clear rationale for owning. Having conviction in your investments means "buying into" a philosophy or system of thought. In order to invest with conviction, you typically need to understand the approach that is being taken. That conviction and understanding is what will allow you to have the type of fortitude common in all successful investors.

An effective investment strategy will take into account a type of contingency thinking which anticipates events that have a low probability of happening but also a devastating effect if they do happen. For instance, portfolios should have some element of protection against a hyper-inflationary scenario. Out-of the-money put options on bonds are one way to do that. It is beyond the scope of this book to delve into the mechanics of this approach, but it is a way to protect the portfolio against a low probability/high expense event similar to the function of homeowners insurance or an umbrella insurance policy.

Less complex ways of hedging against more extreme scenarios (think something along the lines of the financial crisis of 2008-2009) typically involve alternative investments. We mentioned alternative investments previously in the "mulch" section. Generally speaking, alternatives are used because they have a low or negative correlation to stocks and other "traditional" investments, which means they tend to zig when most other investments zag. Most alternative investments fall into one of two categories:

- Alternative Asset Classes – These invest using traditional methodologies (i.e., buy and hold) but in asset classes other than stocks, bonds, or cash. Some examples here would include commodities, real estate, and precious metals.
- Alternative Strategies – These are either traditional or alternative investment classes which use less conventional investment techniques. Examples here would be long/short strategies and managed futures.

The choice of alternative investments available to investors is growing. Currently, they are more accessible than ever through recent product innovation, such as their introduction into mutual funds and exchange-traded funds. This trend is sure to continue going forward, as investments that are now considered "alternatives" will become more assimilated into traditional portfolios.

While alternative investments can be a great way to mitigate market risk by providing further diversification and a hedge against volatility, these are also potentially very confusing investments. The theme we mentioned previously should be applied here even more rigorously: Understand your investments. If you do not know how they work – or an advisor cannot explain it to you in plain English in a few sentences –

then the best advice is to run the other way. "Trust me" is not a path to a successful investment strategy.

[6]

Establish Proper Benchmarks

After considering goals and potential risks, it is essential to establish the appropriate benchmarks. Typical benchmark discussions involve the comparison of "relative" versus "absolute" portfolio returns, but that shouldn't be the main focus.

The focus should be your goals – whether you can retire as planned, gift to your children or buy that vacation home. Life goals are what matter the most. So investment performance should be analyzed through a lens of whether it's enabling you to achieve your specific goals. Knowing that your portfolio is down less than the overall stock market index is little consolation when the market is being pummeled and you find out that you will have to work another three years to retire as a result.

Toward the end of 2008 and into early 2009, the stock market had suffered the most severe decline since the Great Depression. At its lowest point, the broad stock market was down 50% from its peak. Because it was due to a global economic downturn and a financial meltdown, hardly any areas of the economy were spared. Therefore, nearly every investor lost money. And the more you had in stocks, the more money you lost.

So it was not uncommon for the following conversation to occur between clients and their financial advisors:

Client: How is my account doing?

Advisor: Well, it's held up pretty well all things considered. You've lost about 30% from the peak.

Client: 30%? And that's good?! How do you figure that?

Advisor: Well the S&P 500 (stock index) is down almost 50% so compared to that you're doing pretty well since about 2/3rd's of your portfolio is in stocks...

Client: (Sigh)

What's going on here? Typically, the client and the advisor have different benchmarks. An advisor, being in the business, evaluates performance on a relative basis. The portfolio composition is broken down into risky (stocks) and less risky (bonds) categories and evaluated based on how those specific investments held up as compared to their overall market indices. This is relative performance benchmarking and is how investment performance has traditionally been analyzed and evaluated.

Relative performance works fine when the markets are relatively stable or doing well. So, during the 18 year bull market from 1982 through 2000, relative performance became the norm and no one really complained. Since that time, things have changed. Two of the worst bear markets in history have occurred since the millennium. The tech bubble in early 2000's was a concentrated downturn which was mostly contained within a particular sector of the economy. So, business as usual persisted on Wall Street.

2008 changed everything. We have a new world order: an interdependent, global economy that provides the potential for significant volatility unlike anything we've seen before. As a result, the old model of benchmarking to relative performance doesn't work anymore. Investors need a different benchmark: one that relates to their goals. The implication is each investor needs a customized benchmark based on his or her financial goals and future income needs.

To properly evaluate investments and make informed investment decisions on an ongoing basis, you need one thing in particular: context. What does a loss of this magnitude mean for your financial situation? How does it relate to your goals? Are you still able to meet your income needs? If yes, you can afford to weather the downturn. If no, you may need to make some changes.

But the point is you can put it into context. You have a framework to answer the questions: "How does this affect me?" and "What now?" Having a plan in place that connects life goals with portfolio allocation enables you to be proactive rather than reactive when it comes to financial decision making.

[7]

Portfolio Construction

Now that you have established goals, defined risk and set the proper benchmarks, it's time to construct the portfolio. Portfolio construction is defined around long-term needs and goals. It reflects current income needs and future cash flow requirements (e.g., educational expenses, health care needs, retirement and gifting goals). The goal-based benchmark will provide guidance as to how much market risk must be taken in order to succeed. The higher the benchmark performance goal, the greater the market risk of the portfolio; and vice versa.

Portfolios are constructed for the long term and designed with a strategic asset allocation to address the individual's needs. Most portfolios include a mix of actively-managed and passive strategies, which are designed to lessen market risk while at the same time pursuing areas offering stronger relative returns.

The increasing availability of alternative asset classes, which can enhance overall portfolio return and risk metrics by investing in assets and strategies that have lower correlations to stocks and bonds, are also producing changes in strategic allocations.

Strategic allocations by their nature tend to change more slowly unless there is a change in an individual's needs or risk profile. When changes occur, they often reflect large-scale national or worldwide events that change the overall market outlook for various asset classes and their associated risk and return characteristics.

Within this strategic framework, tactical allocations may be used to respond to current or anticipated market fluctuations. Tactical strategies are typically implemented with a 6 to 12 month time horizon although the decisions are monitored on an ongoing basis to ensure they remain consistent with the outlook and rationale for implementing them. History suggests that even modest tactical changes can have a meaningful and positive effect on overall returns.

What happens with new money you are investing? We talked about "sprinkler systems." What is the best way to invest recurring cash transfers that will be added to an account?

Dollar-cost averaging is the term for an effective method of investing which allows you to actually take advantage of the volatility of the investment markets. The natural human tendency is to buy more stock when prices are rising and stop buying as prices fall. Dollar-cost averaging forces you to do the opposite. You end up buying the most stock when prices are low.

Here's how it works: Suppose you invest $600 per month into a mutual fund in your 401(k) plan. If a share of the fund costs $60 in October, you buy 10 shares. If the price falls to $40 in November, you buy 15 shares. If the price then climbs to $75, you buy 8 shares. The bottom line is that the average share price ($58.33) was higher that what you paid for each share ($54.55). The chart on the next page shows this example.

Dollar-Cost Averaging in a Volatile Market			
	Investment Each Month	Share Price	Shares Purchased
	$600	$60	10
	$600	$40	15
	$600	$75	8
Total	$1,800	$175	33
	Average Share Cost:	$54.55	($1,800/33)
	Average Share Price:	$58.33	($175/3)

Though it may cushion your losses somewhat, dollar-cost averaging does not protect you from a falling investment. But the strategy does ensure that you invest more new money when prices are low so you can enjoy the increase when the market recovers.

[8]

Buckets of Money

One practical method for making wise investment decisions is to use what we'll call the buckets of money concept. This approach creates a useful framework for investment decision-making, particularly for those approaching retirement. The idea is to divide financial resources into different categories based on the intent that money is to be used for.

Least Risk/Return   Most Risk/Return

Income	Income	Growth	Growth
Liquid	Not Liquid	Liquid	Not Liquid

The buckets concept helps to more clearly delineate between "growth" investments and "safer" investments. The two buckets on the left can serve primarily as a source of income and wealth preservation. If income needs in retirement are met exclusively from investments held in the income buckets, then the other two growth buckets on the right side

.n fluctuate with the equity markets without affecting one's ability to meet ongoing living expenses. They are meant to serve as a hedge against the rising costs of living by keeping up with or surpassing the inflation rate. This helps answer a fundamental, yet important question on the minds of most people nearing retirement:

How do I "get paid" after I stop working? In other words, what are the mechanics of retirement income planning?

Understanding the intentions of different buckets of money and where your income will be derived can provide a valuable tool for avoiding emotionally-driven decisions that sabotage your investment strategy.

The best investors have typically been contrarians. Successful investors are worried not when everyone is worried but when essentially no one is worried. They love the opportunity presented in situations where panic is full blown and conditions appear utterly certain to get worse. The central imperative of investing – buy low, sell high – is implying a contrarian approach.

It is easy to say the words "buy low and sell high," but it is very difficult to follow through with that strategy in the midst of severe volatility in either direction. When things are going well and stock prices are at their highest, the headlines are positive and investors are feeling optimistic and hopeful. That is the best time to sell. On the other hand, the time to buy is when everything seems gloomy. Emotions – greed on the upside and fear on the downside – are powerful drivers that are hard to overcome.

In May of 1932, Dean Witter said:

> *"Some people say they want to wait for a clearer view of the future. But when the future is again clear, the present bargains will have vanished. In fact does anyone think that today's prices will prevail once full confidence has been restored?"*

He said those words just weeks before the end of the worst bear market in history. And if ever there was a time for investors to sit on the sidelines and wait until things improve, that would have seemingly been the time to do so. The fact is there is a strong tendency to follow our emotions: sell low and buy high and thereby ensure horrible investment results.

The reality is that it is only with hindsight that we can know the high or low points of a market cycle. And, to the extent we do try to time the market, we are emotional beings whose emotions are going to dictate the exact opposite of what is in our financial best interest during times of market volatility. So, what should we do? Nothing to change the long term strategy; realize that time is one of our biggest assets.

Staying the course with money that is already invested and systematically investing new money with a dollar-cost averaging program are proven methods of achieving superior investment performance. So the best advice is usually to tune out the constant barrage of negativity filling most of our 24 hour news cycle. Once you've established your goals, developed a thoughtful plan to achieve them, and implemented an investment strategy, you can improve your odds of success by resisting the urge to make changes and let it be. In other words when in doubt, don't just do something, stand there.

[9]

Insurance

Earlier, we talked about market risk and inflation risk. Another major source of risk is mortality risk. Much of our planning assumes that we are alive to carry it out. Obviously, premature death or disability can wreck even the best plans if we do not consider those consequences. This takes us back to the main concept of Section 1: Human Capital.

In terms of financial decision-making, people think almost exclusively in terms of what they already have, such as stocks, bonds, real estate, cash, or other investments. Yet the reality is that often times the single biggest component of overall wealth is not the stuff that we own; it's ourselves and our ability to earn income in the future. The term for this is human capital.

Human capital is the collective skills, knowledge, or other intangible assets of individuals that can be used to create a meaningful economic impact. This concept is relatively straightforward. You earn income over time based on your labor and personal efforts. All of that future income that will be accumulated over the years can be quantified. With this methodology, the current value of your human capital is simply the net present value of all the earnings you are expected to receive over your lifetime.

For example, if a person were starting a 40-year career with an initial salary of $40,000, and expected her salary to grow at an average annual rate of 3%, then using a 7% rate for the time value of money, this person's human capital at the start of her career will be approximately $700,000. (This is the net present value of the future income stream in today's dollars.)

Higher growth rates or lower time value of money rates will lead to higher values of human capital. It is not uncommon for the human capital of many new college graduates to exceed $1 million.

It is imperative that we assign a financial value to each family member's human capital. For those of us who are not yet retired or financially independent, we must consider others who are dependent on our earned income. These survivors could be spouses, children, grandchildren, or other relatives or friends.

What we are really trying to discern is the need for insurance to replace the earned income relied on to meet financial needs in the instance of disability or death. As we get older, earnings will typically increase along with specialized knowledge and skill levels. However, our need for insurance will decline over time because we are increasing our assets (through savings and investments).

With insurance we are seeking to fill a gap between future earned income and our accumulated investment assets. As we approach financial independence, the gap closes between our human capital (income) and our financial capital (assets). This is illustrated in the following chart.

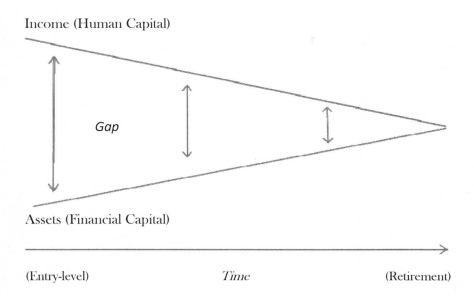

Income (Human Capital)

Gap

Assets (Financial Capital)

(Entry-level)　　　　　　*Time*　　　　　　(Retirement)

When looking through the lens of human capital, the accumulation of assets over time does not really represent the creation of financial capital from saving. Instead, it is the *conversion of human capital to financial capital.*

When an individual starts his/her career, there is a certain amount of income that will be earned during life; as that income actually is earned the client slowly converts potential future income into current income, and in the process either spends that income or saves it. If it is spent, it's consumed; if it is not, it is saved and contributes to financial capital.

Financial capital in turn is invested to earn and grow so that it will be available for consumption in the future (i.e., in retirement). As a result, you could say that everything flows from your human capital; it is either income you consume, or income you convert into financial capital so that it can be consumed later.

Financial independence basically means that you have accumulated sufficient assets to create a sustainable stream of income to meet your required living expenses. That is the point at which the two lines intersect, implying you have converted enough of your human capital into financial capital to meet your financial goals.

In other words, you can replace what had been earned income with cash flow from your investment portfolio. In order to determine how much you (will) need to be financially independent, we will now turn to the Retirement Scorecard and show how that can be calculated.

[10]

Retirement Planning

Even though the word is poorly defined and understood, retirement is the lynchpin of financial planning. All other financial planning decisions need to be made in relation to their effects on your retirement goals (a.k.a. your plan for financial independence).

To illustrate the centrality of retirement planning, consider the previous topic regarding insurance. In order to calculate life insurance needs, you need to know how much you will need to be financially independent. In determining how much to allocate to the different "buckets" of money, you need to know how much income you will need from the portfolio in retirement. To determine the optimal amount to save for children's education or to give away for charitable purposes, you need to know your own "number"; again and again it comes down to funding your own financial independence.

There are a number of different ways to calculate your retirement needs, but I think it's most helpful to break it into two broad categories: linear analysis and probability analysis. Let's start with the latter: Probability analysis – sometimes referred to as Monte Carlo or Stochastic Modeling – is a complicated methodology using statistical modeling tools. This type of approach applies scientific rigor to the process. It is most helpful when the number or range of variables has been reduced and a transition may be imminent.

This is often the case with someone on the verge of transitioning into retirement or making some other major financial decision. In those cases, a probability analysis which runs a simulation of hundreds or even thousands of iterations can make sense.

For instance, a portfolio with an 8% average rate of return might fluctuate primarily between –8% and 24% based on historical fluctuations. Probability analysis commonly runs a thousand simulations of future outcomes within the specified range.

The most useful result of this number-crunching activity is determining the probability of achieving one's financial goals. You can then take it a step further to determine the effects of changes in variables over which you have control (i.e., spending amounts and investment allocation).

But while probability analysis can be helpful in the right circumstances, it should really be a secondary step applied when necessary. It is almost like getting a "second-opinion" on a medical condition to see if the diagnosis remains the same or "stress-testing" your plan to see if it will hold up when tested against adverse historical market conditions.

What is needed initially – and for some it will be the only retirement planning needed – is a linear analysis. A linear analysis is a simpler methodology which assumes averages. For instance, average rate of return, an average inflation rate, and a specified life expectancy. Since linear analysis is a more efficient way to calculate retirement needs and also a good starting point, we will use that methodology in the calculator we'll be using here. It's what we'll refer to as a "Retirement Scorecard."

But first I should say something about the shortcoming of this methodology. The stock market almost never delivers an average return; it varies greatly from year to year. Similarly, inflation rates can vary quite a bit from whatever average rate is assumed.

One way to counter that shortcoming of linear methodology is to use conservative assumptions or to interpret the results conservatively. In other words, if the long term average return of a balanced portfolio (50% stocks / 50% bonds) is 7.5% pre-tax, you might want to assume 6% and see if the plan still "works." Or, if you use 7.5%, do not look for results that "just barely" qualify as "successful" but target results that are in the safer range so that there is some "buffer" or excess capital available to withstand future market volatility.

On the next page is a Retirement Scorecard. The first thing to do is enter information into all of the shaded boxes. The first three numbers you will need to enter are three basic assumptions: inflation, rate of return, and years until retirement. If you are already retired, just enter zero. For inflation, the long term historical average is approximately 3%. You can enter 4% if you want to be conservative. The rate of return assumption is pre-tax. You should enter 6%, 7%, or 8%. The basic rule of thumb here is that the more aggressive you are (i.e., higher stock allocation), the higher the return assumption you can justify.

The next entry is annual expenses. This is your estimate of what you'll need to spend in retirement every year; not including taxes. While there are rules of thumb around spending in retirement being a portion of current living expenses (sometimes 80%), my experience is that people who are healthy in retirement end up spending at least as much as they did pre-retirement so I would suggest using current living expenses as a good default number. You will enter the spending amount in today's dollars and we will adjust for inflation.

Also under "Income and Expenses" is a list of future income sources. If any of these apply, go ahead and enter those numbers. These should be entered as the actual amounts you expect to receive. In other words, input amounts adjusted for inflation.

Retirement Scorecard

Basic Assumptions

1 Inflation Assumption
2 Return Assumption
3 Years Until Retirement

Income and Expenses	Now	Multiplier	At Retirement

4 Annual Expenses
   Look up Inflation Multiplier (#1 and #3)
5 Annual Income In Retirement (input below)
   a) Work
   b) Pensions
   c) Social Security
   d) Real Estate
   e) Gifts
   f) Other
   TOTAL ('a' through 'f' above)

6 Net Income Needed From Portfolio
   Expenses (#4) minus TOTAL Income (#5)
7 Adjust Income Need (above) to Account for Taxes
   Multiply #6 by 1.25% (assuming 25% effective rate)

Investments

8 Investment Assets (Total)
   Look up ROR Multiplier (#2 and #3)
9 Annual Savings
   Look up Savings Multiplier (#2 and #3)
10 Projected Total Investments at Retirement
   Add #8 and #9

Evaluation

11 Withdrawal Rate
   Total Income Needed (#7) / Total Investments (#10)

12 Score (see below for self-assessment & interpretation)

If withdrawal rate is below 3.0%:   A (consider gifting & tax planning for excess wealth)
If withdrawal rate ranges from 3-4%:   B (likely a stable & sustainable plan)
If withdrawal rate ranges from 4-5%:   C (continue to monitor & strive for lower end of range)
If withdrawal rate ranges from 5-6%:   D (unlikely to meet your goals; reassess)
If withdrawal rate is above 6%:   F (unsustainable for long term; revisit assumptions)

The last two inputs are total assets and total ongoing savings. Total assets should include all investable assets such as retirement accounts, bank accounts, and investment accounts. It should also include illiquid assets which are earmarked for retirement purposes. These would be things like net business interest and investment real estate. Primary residence or personal property should not be included here.

Next you will want to look up "multipliers" in the Appendix ("Table of Multipliers" on page 219). There are three boxes in this column: Annual Expenses (4), Investment Assets (8), and Annual Savings (9). The "At Retirement" boxes next to each of these multipliers can then by filled in as well by multiplying the number on the left (in each of the shaded boxes) by the multiplier next to it.

The remainder of the boxes in the "At Retirement" column can then be calculated based on instructions provided on the scorecard. The last box to complete on the sheet is the score itself. There are ranges that you can reference to determine your score. The score is akin to a grade: A, B, C, D, or F.

However, do not be as alarmed as you might have been when receiving a lower grade in school. There are very few people who receive an "A" and a whole lot who get D's and F's. That is just the reality of how difficult it can be to achieve financial independence. If your score is on the lower end of the spectrum, the most helpful thing will be to re-evaluate some assumptions. What if you saved more? What if you spent less? What if you add a future income source like working in retirement? See how the score changes accordingly.

If, on the other hand, you have a score of an "A", you might want to get more conservative with your assumptions (i.e., lower the rate of return or increase your spending assumption or reduce amounts of income available in retirement). If the score remains high, then you know you've got a very strong plan and may even want to reduce your total investment assets to gauge how much you may be able to give away without jeopardizing your own financial independence.

If you need further assistance in completing the Retirement Scorecard or if you would just like to see what a completed one looks like, there is a sample in the Appendix. Please note the scorecard is meant only as a rough gauge to help determine if you are on the right track and if your goals are reasonable. Consider working with a professional advisor before making any major decisions.

[11]

Estate Planning

In terms of our central metaphor, the presumption is that while you are alive, you are the gardener. When you pass away, who tends to it and what tools can they use? This is the concern of estate planning: the process by which an individual or family arranges the transfer of assets in anticipation of death.

Wills and Trusts

The will is the most basic tool of estate planning. It is essential to have a will drafted. A will shows how your property will be distributed at death, who administers your estate, and who cares for minor children.

Additionally, your situation may dictate the need for a trust. A trust is a document that spells out rules you want followed for property held in trust for your beneficiaries. Trusts can help you avoid or reduce estate tax liability, protect assets, avoid probate, and exert more control over the transition of property to your heirs.

Trustee

The role of a trustee is to adhere to the terms of the trust document and fulfill its objectives. A trustee can be an individual or corporate entity. A trustee has many specific duties including the preservation, protection, and investment of trust assets. Other duties include loyalty to the beneficiaries, clear and accurate record keeping regarding inflows, outflows, and investment gains and losses. A trustee may need to sell assets, manage property, or continue a business if necessary. It is often important that the trustee relate well to beneficiaries and be flexible to changing needs.

Power of Attorney

A Durable Power of Attorney (DPOA) is a tool that allows someone to carry on your financial affairs and protect property in a period of incapacity. When appointing someone to serve as DPOA, you want it to be a person you trust to manage your financial affairs while you are unable. If permitted in your state, you can name more than one person, either as alternatives or as partners. You can make these "attorney-in-fact" powers as broad or as limited as you want. Also, you can change or terminate your DPOA as long as you have retained capacity to do so.

Executor (or Personal Representative)

The executor of an estate (in some states referred to as the personal representative) is the person named in the will to administer instructions according to the final wishes of the deceased. The executor should be someone you can trust, has a close relationship to your family, and has some understanding of business and tax laws. A family member or close friend may seem like the best choice, but you should also be aware of the stress and logistics of this role. Preparing and filing tax returns, obtaining appraisals, and accurate accounting are typical responsibilities that an executor needs to ensure are completed.

Guardian

If you have minor children, the most important decision you'll make with regards to an estate plan is typically who to appoint to take care of your children if you die. It is crucial to ask the potential guardian whether he or she is willing to act as your children's guardian. It is wise to appoint a back-up guardian in case your initial choice cannot or will not serve for whatever reason.

Account Titling

It is crucial to make sure that assets are titled in a manner that will fulfill your wishes of how you want to provide for your beneficiaries. For instance, you may want to avoid the additional administrative costs and lack of privacy associated with probate (the court process of settling an estate). If so, revocable trusts can be an effective way to directly transfer assets to your beneficiaries and avoid probate.

Beneficiary designations for qualified retirement plans and life insurance should be reviewed and synchronized with your estate plan. If individuals are named as beneficiaries on these types of assets, they will receive these assets without having to go through the probate process.

Ongoing Considerations

For all of these aforementioned roles, you want to make sure that you have communicated your intentions to your appointed representatives (trustee, POA, guardian, executor) to make sure that they are in agreement to act in this capacity and feel comfortable doing so. It is essential to review your estate plan and update it on a regular basis as dictated by changes in circumstances (i.e., birth of a child, change in marital status, changes in relationships or intentions). Also, it is advisable to educate and communicate to the family in advance your intentions with regard to your estate. Studies show that those individuals prepared to inherit wealth will more wisely steward those assets than those who are not prepared to inherit.

For a more in-depth discussion about estate planning (particularly with regards to tax minimization, gifting, and charitable planning strategies) see "Advanced Estate Planning" in the Appendix.

[12]

Retirement Revisited

In Section I, we discussed the importance of redefining retirement so that it is more about "retiring to" something instead of merely "retiring from." Retirement in this sense does not necessitate a change in lifestyle. In fact, for some people who love the work they do, their lives may look remarkably similar in retirement as they looked before retirement. The key difference is financial independence.

If you are financially independent, you may still work. But, in that case, you are working because you want to; not because you have to. The lifting of financial burdens when attaining financial independence can be quite freeing. It can also allow for considerable human capital to be harnessed.

Consider the possibilities if you were to remove all financial constraints from your vocational aspirations. This is a great opportunity to dream and envision the great things you can do in the next stage of life (assuming you are not there already). Contemplate the vast array of opportunities you could have if there were no major "practical" financial concerns weighing you down.

I mentioned the concept of financial independence, and I think it's useful in the narrower sense strictly pertaining to discussions around retirement planning. But ironically it tends to be the financially independent clients I work with who realize most clearly that they are not truly independent. They are grateful for the success they've had and know that many factors contributed to that success. They also tend to realize that a whole lot of other people are less fortunate and may not have been afforded the same opportunities so they are often anxious to give back.

The better word is actually *financial interdependence*. That more accurately portrays the reality of our economic system. The story that remains to be written is not merely the trillions of dollars that baby boomers will be rolling over for their own retirement. But rather, I look forward to the tale of great social enterprise to be propelled into motion by a huge investment of financial capital as well as vast human capital as these mentally and physically healthy baby boomers redefine what "retirement" really means.

Section IV

SOCIAL CAPITAL: "The Fruit"

"The true meaning of life is to plant trees, under whose shade you do not expect to sit." – Nelson Henderson

[1]

Self-Made Mythology

There is much to admire in the idea of the "self-made" man or woman. Everyone appreciates the rags-to-riches stories. The person who comes from nothing to rise to the top, overcoming huge obstacles to reach his goals. The Benjamin Franklin archetype who, as the son of a candle maker, goes on to become a founding father, inventor, and diplomat. It's the essence of the American Dream.

But there is a problem with this story. It's not quite true. It leaves out a lot and takes many things for granted. In his book *Outliers*, Malcolm Gladwell delves into the true reasons for the success of all sorts of famous people – from star athletes to legendary musicians to Silicon Valley billionaires and so on. The essence of what he discovers flies in the face of our fancied versions of the Self-Made Man. He concludes:[1]

> *"People don't rise from nothing...It makes a difference where and when we grew up. The culture we belong to and the legacies passed down by our forebears shape the patterns of our achievement in ways we cannot begin to imagine."*

Winston Churchill said it well:[2]

"Chance, Fortune, Fate, Providence, seem to me only different ways of expressing the same thing, to wit, that a man's own contribution to his life story is continually dominated by an external superior power."

You could be the most intelligent, most talented and creative person ever to step foot on this planet, but if you were born on a mountain in Mongolia in the 12th Century, you would never have achieved anything closely resembling our modern idea of success.

This brings us to a central question: What is our attitude toward our money? How do we define that fundamental relationship? If we cannot claim sole responsibility for any financial good fortune we experience in our lives, then we do not essentially "own" it. We are instead "stewards" of all that we have.

A steward is like a trustee of an account who manages another's property, finances, or other affairs. We are entrusted with managing the gifts we have been given. (These gifts include unique talents and abilities as well as financial resources.)

Stewardship is personal responsibility for taking care of another person's property or financial affairs. It is also the theological belief that humans are responsible for the world, and ought to take care of it.

We can learn a lot about this concept of stewardship by looking at other cultures around the world that are much less individualistic than ours. For instance, in Africa, the concept of "ubuntu" is a central value. Ubuntu can be hard to define but it basically connotes an openness and availability to others. It's a social ethic that focuses on people's allegiances and relations with each other. A person with ubuntu knows that he or she belongs to a greater whole and is diminished when others are humiliated, tortured, or oppressed.

Andrew Carnegie was echoing these ideas when he asserted:[3]

"Surplus wealth is a sacred trust which its possessor is bound to administer in his lifetime for the good of the community."

That is the definition of good stewardship. It also encapsulates the essence of ubuntu. This all leads us to the idea of "social capital."

According to John Field,[4] the concept of social capital starts with the acknowledgement that "relationships matter." The central idea is that "social networks are a valuable asset." Interaction enables people to build communities, to commit themselves to each other, and to knit the social fabric.

What does a culture with strong social capital look like? Well, there is now a range of evidence that communities with a good "stock" of such social capital are more likely to benefit from lower crime figures, better health, higher educational achievement, and better economic growth.[5]

But aside from practical benefits, building social capital also fulfills internal desires embedded within all of us at some level. In his Pulitzer Prize winning book *The Denial of Death*, Ernest Becker says:[6]

"The one thing that has always amazed man is his own inner yearning to be good, an inner sensitivity about the 'way things ought to be' and an excruciatingly warm and melting attraction toward beauty, goodness, and perfection."

Theologian Cornelius Plantinga similarly described this "inner yearning":[7]

"The webbing together of God, humans, and all creation in justice, fulfillment, and delight is what the Hebrew prophets call shalom. We call it peace but it means more than mere peace of mind or a ceasefire between enemies. In the Bible, shalom means universal flourishing, wholeness, and delight – a rich state of affairs in which natural needs are satisfied and natural gifts fruitfully employed... Shalom, in other words, is the way things ought to be."

Those are beautiful pictures invoking love, peace, and beauty... And yet, notice the phrase "the way things *ought to be.*" It's definitely not "the way things *are.*"

In his pioneering study, *Bowling Alone: The Collapse and Revival of American Community*, Harvard political scientist Robert Putnam shows how social bonds are the most powerful predictor of life satisfaction. Unfortunately, his conclusions are not very uplifting. His research concludes that social capital is deteriorating at many different levels. Putnam writes:[8]

> *"Henry Ward Beecher's advice a century ago to 'multiply picnics' is not entirely ridiculous today. We should do this, ironically, not because it will be good for America — though it will be — but because it will be good for us."*

He has found an overall decline in social capital in America over the past fifty years, a trend that may have significant implications for American society.

There is a real danger here that Putnam is pointing toward. A healthy garden is reliant on growing flowers and fruit that can supply mature seeds for new plants. Without fruit, there are no new plants. Indeed, social capital is the "fruit."

Thus, without social capital, we have a dis-integration of society. The fabric that holds us all together begins to unravel and physical, emotional, and spiritual health suffers as a result. Without that strong social fabric, trust decays and at a certain point, this decay begins to manifest itself in serious social problems.

So, how would we see evidence of this type of deterioration in social capital played out?

[2]

Unraveling of the Social Fabric

Politics is one area where we can see it. Regardless of where you stand on the ideological spectrum, it's hard to see anything but dysfunction currently. Despite being the leading country in the free world, the United States seems to now be a civilization that is incapable of governing and reaching decisions on big issues.

Whether it is tax laws expiring, huge entitlement systems headed for bankruptcy, or a looming debt crisis, we do not seem to have elected leaders who are willing and able to talk with one another to solve serious issues. In terms of sheer dysfunction and complete lack of trust across the political aisle, it is hard to recall a situation much worse than the current environment.

Of course, the business world is also suffering from a lack of trust. Since the financial crisis in 2008, the reputation of MBAs – particularly those from the country's elite business schools – has suffered greatly. An overarching sense of public distrust and contempt has built up substantially.

Many have placed the blame for the financial meltdown squarely at the feet of Wall Street and, more specifically, at the Harvard MBAs who were largely responsible for creating so-called "financial weapons of mass destruction" at the big investment banking firms.

This is not an isolated phenomenon. Today's business professionals rank amongst the least trusted members of society and this is a distinction my profession has earned through decades of missteps. From the Savings & Loan Crisis in the 80's to Enron & Worldcom to Bernie Madoff — our community of "leaders" have made mistakes that are unacceptable to shareholders, to employees, to customers, and to society as a whole.

Of course, it's always easy to point fingers. But in many ways, we – as a society – are merely reaping what we've sown. Peggy Noonan explained it well:[9]

> *"In a way, the world is a great liar. It shows you it worships and admires money, but at the end of the day it doesn't, not really. The world admires, and wants to hold on to, and not lose, goodness. It admires virtue. At the end it gives its greatest tributes to generosity, honesty, courage, mercy, talents well used, talents that, brought into this world, make it better. That's what it really admires. That's what we talk about in eulogies, because that's what's important."*

[3]

Redefining the Bottom Line

In 2001, *NY Times* columnist and author David Brooks spent some
time on the campus of Princeton University in order to get to know
some of the future leaders of this country. What he found was a class
of students that was well-liked overall and compared favorably with
many preceding generations of students in terms of their behavior and
work ethic. Brooks observed:[12]

> *"Today's elite college students don't live in that age of rebellion
> and alienation. They grew up in a world in which the countercul-
> ture and the mainstream culture have merged with, and co-opted,
> each other.... They've mostly known parental protection, prosperi-
> ty, and peace."*

Generally, the students had remarkably good relations with their parents and teachers, but something was missing. He explained it this way:

> *"One sometimes has the sense that all the frantic efforts to regulate
> safety, to encourage academic achievement, and to keep busy are
> ways to compensate for missing conceptions of character and vir-
> tue. Not having a vocabulary to discuss what is good and true,*

> *people can at least behave well. It's hard to know what eternal life means, but if you don't smoke you can have long life. It's hard to imagine what it would be like to be a saint, but it's easy to see what it is to be a success."*

Brooks concludes that:

> *"Instead of virtue we talk about accomplishment."*

We tend to think and act as if the mere attainment of goals is all that matters. Or, in Brooks' words, we focus narrowly on "success" and "accomplishment." That's why financial planning has traditionally focused solely on the idea of helping clients reach their financial goals, implying that the nature of the goals is inconsequential. The typical notion is that if you value something and attain it, you're better off as a function of reaching that goal.

A group of social scientists recently challenged that premise. The researchers questioned a group of soon-to-be grads from the University of Rochester about their life goals and then followed up early in their careers to track progress.[13] They divided students into two groups as determined by the nature of their goals:

- Group 1: Those with "extrinsic aspirations" (i.e., become wealthy, famous)

- Group 2: Those with "intrinsic aspirations" (i.e., help others improve their lives, to learn, grow)

Those in Group 1 - focused on accumulating wealth and acquiring acclaim - had levels of self-esteem, and subjective well-being equivalent to when they were students. And not only did their attainment of those extrinsic goals not lead to an increase in well-being, but these recent grads actually showed increases in anxiety, depression, and other negative emotions. Again, these findings are for those students that were actually *successful* in attaining their goals.

Those in Group 2 – the group with more intrinsic aspirations - consistently reported higher levels of subjective well-being 1-2 years later in follow up interviews. This, too, applied to those in the group that successfully attained their goals.

The conclusion is that true happiness depends not merely on having and achieving goals, but having and achieving *the right goals.* There are goals that – if and when they are attained – may actually make you worse off as a result. This is akin to the classic "ladder" analogy. If your goal is to climb to the top of a ladder, it's of little satisfaction to know you've reached the top when you discover it's leaning against the wrong wall.

One intriguing development that has occurred in the aftermath of the global financial crisis was the introduction of the "MBA Oath" by Harvard Business School. The Oath states,[10]

> *"As a manager, my purpose is to serve the greater good by bringing people and resources together to create value that no single individual can build alone."*

By using "my purpose" rather than "one of my main purposes," the oath suggests that *the* primary purpose of the MBA grad is "to serve the greater good." In so doing, it is reasonable to imply that serving the "greater good" takes precedence over individual or corporate success. "Greater good" usually points to the condition of society as a whole.

The oath *seems* to be saying that the primary purpose of work is to benefit society as a whole, and not simply to make money, to find personal fulfillment, or even to enrich my shareholders. This is begging every one of us – hearers and signers of the oath alike – to ask a central question. What is my bottom line? Money? Or is money just a tool used to fulfill a bigger vision?

I do believe that these goals can be compatible. In other words, businesses can thrive and make a positive difference in society. Over the years, I have worked with many business owners who have done just that. They have created wealth, employed significant numbers of people, and sold products that benefited the local community.

But the issue of a bottom line is important. In fact, it is essential. Whether or not we are cognizant of it, our de-facto bottom line is what allows us to prioritize what is really important. So that when the inevitable conflicts of interest arise, we have a filter for making decisions that align with our values.

Regardless of whether or not the oath will actually do any good or have any real effect, the mere fact that this conversation is happening is a good thing. We are broaching the topic of what responsibility business leaders should have to society. A broader vision of the role of business in society is very much welcomed. As Jack Welch had said years ago, "shareholder value is a result, not a strategy." He elaborated by saying that "Your main constituencies are your employees, your customers and your products."

The School of Business and Economics at Seattle Pacific University advocates that its students aspire to find "another way of doing business," in which profit is not the ultimate bottom line.[11]

> *"[I]n the School of Business and Economics (SBE), we start with the premise that the purpose of business is to serve. In particular, it is to serve the community by providing the goods and services that will enable the community to flourish (an external goal). It also serves by providing meaningful and creative work that will allow employees to express aspects of their identity on the job (an internal goal)."*

The consensus of findings here and elsewhere points toward the need for overarching goals and values that facilitate meaning and purpose by serving others in the community and enabling it to flourish. In other words, building social capital through an investment of our time, talents, and resources is a central element to finding individual fulfillment. The key element in all of this is the idea of service, which is one of those ideas more effectively understood through illustration than definition.

[4]

Service Exemplified

"Am I not destroying my enemies when I make friends of them?"

– Abraham Lincoln

In her Pulitzer Prize winning book about Abraham Lincoln called *Team of Rivals*, Doris Kearns Goodwin explained how Lincoln appointed all of his fiercest opponents and political rivals to his top cabinet posts after he was elected President.[14]

As a testament to Lincoln's character, he was able to form true friendships with most of these former rivals. But if there was one member of President Lincoln's Cabinet with whom he was not particularly friendly, it was Salmon Chase. Chase had opposed Lincoln for the Republican nomination for President and was subsequently appointed Treasury Secretary. He seemed to always have a chip on his shoulder and was constantly feeling ignored or overlooked.

Chase complained frequently to others - generals, journalists, politicians, and friends. Chase let it be known to anyone who would listen that he would be a better President than Lincoln - and thus Chase had real difficulty overcoming his ambition and jealousy to become Mr. Lincoln's friend. In his years as Treasury Secretary, Chase's vanity and sense of superiority seemed to grow.

Chase thought himself far more qualified to serve as President than Lincoln, and he made numerous attempts to undermine Lincoln in order to position himself to run against him in Lincoln's bid for re-election.

The most egregious example was an article that was circulated to one hundred leading Republicans in the North. It was clear that, in all likelihood, Chase was privy to the leak which was a scathing indictment of Lincoln and quoted Chase as saying "the dignity of the nation" would suffer if Lincoln were to be re-elected. In the fallout from some of these unsavory actions toward the President, Chase eventually resigned from his position as Treasury Secretary.

Massachusetts Congressman John B. Alley observed that even after Chase left the Cabinet, "he visited some of his old friends in New England - among others, myself. He was exceedingly bitter and denunciatory of Mr. Lincoln, and so open in his opposition that some of his friends rebuked him." Lincoln biographers John G. Nicolay and John Hay wrote:

> *"Even to comparative strangers he could not write without speaking slightingly of the President."*

Incredibly, President Lincoln did not hold this behavior against Chase. In fact, he ultimately gave the most important nomination of his presidency – the Chief Justice of the Supreme Court – to Salmon Chase. He did not blindly nominate Chase without evaluating alternatives, nor did he blindly reject him. Lincoln had at least two qualified candidates for Chief Justices who were more congenial personally or politically ahead of Chase and yet he opted for the man who had repeatedly tried to sabotage and humiliate him.

Lincoln's handling of his relationship with Chase said a great deal about Mr. Lincoln's notions of relationships in general and friendships in particular. Although he valued friendship, he did not place friendship above the needs of the "public service."

Lincoln's assistant, John Nicolay, perhaps captured the essence of Lincoln's actions best of all:[15]

> *"Probably no other man than Lincoln would have had...the degree of magnanimity to thus forgive and exalt a rival who had so deeply and unjustifiably intrigued against him. It is however only another marked illustration of the greatness of the President."*

[5]

The Patriot

We could all learn a great deal from Lincoln. What inspires such a great dedication to service above all self-interest?

G. K. Chesterton described two "peculiar" creatures – known as the optimist and the pessimist. He argues that neither is quite sufficient. Instead he considers the most appropriate attitude to be more like a military loyalty than to an attitude of either criticism or approval. He calls this an attitude of primary loyalty or what he referred to as "patriotism."

Chesterton captured the essence of this idea of patriotism in the following description:[16]

> *"The point is not that this world is too sad to love or too glad not to love; the point is that when you do love a thing, its gladness is a reason for loving it and its sadness is a reason for loving it more... Similarly, optimism and pessimism are alike arguments for the cosmic patriot."*

The patriot encapsulates the attitudes of both the optimist and pessimist and out of his love for this world, is called to action. In this sense, Lincoln was above all a true patriot.

The opposite of Chesterton's patriot is what I'll call the spectator. We must choose to be either a patriot or a spectator. Western Civilization of the 21st Century is full of spectators. To understand what I mean by "spectator," I should take a step back to give some philosophical context.

Flannery O' Connor correctly pointed out:[17]

> *"If you live today you breathe in nihilism. In or out of the church, it's the gas you breathe."*

She's referring to the prominent denial of the existence of any basis for truth. Nihilism is the idea that there is no reason to prefer one answer to any other. It's essentially a view of the world that lacks hope or meaning due to the absence of truth.

Author Daniel Taylor argues that the spiritual manifestation of nihilism is cynicism. The cynic is ultimately a coward which stems from the intrinsic fear of risking anything. Uninvolved, detached, and apathetic, the cynic approaches life as a spectator. The spectator espouses a false sense of objectivity, but in reality cannot be truly removed from the influences of his/her cultural background, upbringing, and education.[18]

Sadly, it does not take a keen sense of observation to see this cynicism and apathy abounding all around us. Most of us, if we are honest, are probably more cynical than we'd like to admit.

It is not the criticism or the pointing out of problems itself that is the issue. But rather it is what we do with this information. It is much too easy to set into a general apathy and avoid taking positive action. The best way to remedy this tendency toward cynicism is to engage and become committed.

So, why is commitment so difficult? It takes moral courage and conviction. To be committed to something bigger than ourselves, we must feel that there is a right thing to do; a right action to take. Moral ambivalence leads only to passive observance and critique. Moral courage and fortitude are pre-requisites for this particular notion of "patriotism."

I just finished watching the film *Good Will Hunting*. It's probably the tenth time I've seen it, but it affected me in a whole new way this time. Here's my quick take of one of the quintessential relationships of the movie. Matt Damon, who plays the lead character Will, is an arrogant, self-absorbed, disrespectful punk kid. He's also a boy genius – a mathematical prodigy of incredible intellect. Sean, played by Robin Williams, is a therapist whose project it is to turn this boy around.

True to his character, Will debases and denigrates Sean at every opportunity at the onset of their meeting. If Sean were to tell Will to take a flying leap and write him off as a lost cause, he'd have every right. But he doesn't do that, and as a result, it inflicts on him quite a bit of personal anguish. Yet, through the pain he bears, Sean is able to stick with Will and gradually we see a shift in character.

Will, who we discover grew up as an orphan and was abused and beaten by his stepfather, goes through an unnatural change for him in actually beginning to trust and open up to Sean. By the end of this metamorphosis, Will and Sean have both been challenged and stretched, proactively taking on risks and growing as a result.[19]

This is not a new concept, but it's an immensely powerful one. It's a concept I've seen played out countless times in nearly all the epic movies and in the lyrics of some of the greatest songs. I'm talking about redemption. Someone changes and grows and becomes more like the person they were intended to be as a direct result of the willing sacrifice of another person.

And yet, as inspirational as we find these stories of grace and redemption to be, it can be really hard to actually live it out. If you are Robin Williams' character in *Good Will Hunting*, you come to a fork in the road when you meet Matt Damon's character. And it is a whole lot easier to take the road of spectator and just decide to withdraw from the situation and see if someone else can figure out a way to work with this young man.

The uninvolved route is a lot less painful and less risky than it is to be vulnerable and open yourself emotionally only to be ridiculed and disrespected by the one you're trying to help. The "patriot" or active participant is voluntarily choosing to be inflicted with pain in an attempt to help someone who has not done anything to deserve it. It's a free and undeserved gift of grace, which makes it so powerful to observe, but also so hard to actually execute.

Going back to the garden example, plants take in carbon dioxide and give off oxygen. Grace is like oxygen that gives life to human beings. Grace is showing mercy and love to those that don't deserve it. It breaks cycles of anger and hatred and has the capacity to change a whole culture. Grace is life-giving. But it is also painful for the one giving grace. It is unnatural and difficult - at least in the short run.

The fact is unforgiveness and vengeance can feel good initially. If a person has wronged me, I feel he deserves to be punished or at least get a little dose of his own medicine. When we want to get "justice" for ourselves, we want to wrong those who wrong us – or at least withhold our affection and friendship. It seems logical and fair... But there is a cost.

The short term pleasure of this attitude of unforgiveness gives way to something else. It can be hard to see it in ourselves because it's a gradual process, but it's easy to observe it in others. A person who has held a grudge for years is different; changed. His face is a little more distorted and discontent; insides are tensed and knotted up...That person is dying inside; quite literally as well in many cases. Anger has been shown to be the most dangerous of all emotions to our physical health.

That's what the writer Annie Lamont was referring to when she said:[20]

"unforgiveness is like drinking rat poison and expecting the rat to die."

But what does it practically look like to show grace to people and consequently help to build social capital? How do we actually do this? Not just in movies, but in real life.

There may be no better example of this than Martin Luther King, who initiated sweeping social change and rectified the enormous racial injustice through means of non-violent resistance and grace. His own words here perfectly capture the movement he led and his leadership ethos:[21]

"To our most bitter opponents we say: 'We shall match your capacity to inflict suffering by our capacity to endure suffering. We shall meet your physical force with soul force. Do to us what you will, and we shall continue to love you. We cannot in all good conscience obey your unjust laws because noncooperation with evil is as much a moral obligation as is cooperation with good. Throw us in jail and we shall still love you. Bomb our homes and threaten our children, and we shall still love you. Send your hooded perpetrators of violence into our community at the midnight hour and beat us and leave us half dead, and we shall still love you. But be ye assured that we will wear you down by our capacity to suffer. One day we shall win freedom but not only for ourselves. We shall so appeal to your heart and conscience that we shall win you in the process and our victory will be a double victory.'"

[6]

What's Your Story?

As we discussed initially in Section I, we all have stories we live by in order to explain the world. The first story we considered was our understanding of wealth; what it is and where it comes from. We also unpacked our stories regarding our understanding of the words "work" and "retirement." But what about the really big issues? What are the stories we believe about our ultimate purpose and meaning in life? Voice mail messages request two pieces of information:

Who are you?   -- And --   What do you want?

These happen to be two tremendously difficult questions to answer. In other words, what's your story? What's this life all about? What really matters to you?

Andrew Delbanco says it this way:[22]

> *"Human beings need to organize the inchoate sensations amid which we pass our days – pain, desire, pleasure, fear - into a story. When that story leads somewhere and thereby helps us navigate through life to its inevitable terminus in death, it gives us hope."*

Unfortunately, in many ways modern media has taught us to live decontextualized lives. Just as a TV program or website has nothing to do with anything before or after it, nor the commercials or ads inside it, we learn to view life as a series of random, unconnected events which may be entertaining, but bear no significance toward any larger picture.

As a result, many of us have lost the ability to integrate experiences into a larger whole. It is seemingly true that the majority of Americans are content to live without developing any sort of overarching framework or philosophy; life is simply life, and one doesn't need to consider it. In other words, there's no real intentional story. Of course, there is always a default story, but it's much less interesting and fulfilling than it could otherwise be.

Donald Miller perfectly captured this idea when he said the following:[23]

> *"If you watched a movie about a guy who wanted a Volvo and worked years to get it, you wouldn't cry at the end when he drove off the lot, testing the windshield wipers. You wouldn't tell your friends you saw a beautiful movie or go home and put a record on to think about the story you'd seen. The truth is, you wouldn't remember that movie a week later, except you'd feel robbed and want your money back. Nobody cries at the end of a movie about a guy who wants a Volvo.*
>
> *But we spend years actually living those stories, and expect our lives to be meaningful. The truth is, if what we choose to do with our lives won't make a story meaningful, it won't make a life meaningful either..."*

We can all relate to these types of meaningless "stories." Along with the unprecedented prosperity of the Western Civilization of the early 21st Century, many of us have had the opportunity to live comfortable, but unfulfilling lives.

David Foster Wallace is considered by many to have been the greatest writer of recent times. In a 1996 interview with *Salon*, he was asked to explain the idea behind his masterpiece novel, *Infinite Jest*. He said:[24]

> *"...(it is) something that doesn't have very much to do with physical circumstances, or the economy, or any of the stuff that gets talked about in the news. It's more like a stomach-level sadness. I see it in myself and my friends in different ways. It manifests itself in a kind of lostness."*

Robert McKee is a creative writing instructor and author of *Story: Substance, Structure, Style and the Principles of Screenwriting* (what has been called the "Screenwriter's Bible"). In it, McKee writes about the "decline of story" and attributes it primarily to a lack of meaning in modern life.

McKee has suggested:[25]

> *"(the) reason the art of the story is in decline is because we here in the west lead lives of remarkable comfort, with very little effort... This comfort in the west has misled the modern writer to think that's what life is about..."*

He observes that current writers seldom dig beyond the veneer of the external to the deep core where life's truths lie. In essence, the creative writing profession is struggling to develop meaningful scripts in large part because the writers themselves do not possess meaningful scripts by which they live their own lives.

Back to the Wallace interview... he went on to explain what he believed to be the source of what he termed a pervasive "lostness" by stating:[26]

"I get the feeling that a lot of us, privileged Americans, as we enter our early 30's, have to find a way to put away childish things and confront stuff about spirituality and values."

In another interview from 1993, Wallace had surmised,[27]

"This is a generation that has an inheritance of absolutely nothing as far as meaningful moral values."

Wallace – considered to be one of the greatest minds of his generation – hanged himself on September 12, 2008.

He and Robert McKee – great writer and great teacher of writers alike – were both saying the same thing. Our lives (and the stories that reflect them) need to be about something much deeper and more meaningful than what we are being taught to believe in modern culture. It means there is the need for value judgments to be made. There is such a thing as truth, though it's not always easy to discern. And we will only find true fulfillment in life in our search for it. It is through that journey for truth and meaning that we will be able to write and live truly epic stories.

The fact is we all crave to have a sense of purpose and meaning that transcends our own lives. And yet we live in a celebrity-obsessed culture that will barely acknowledge those things amidst all the distractions. Recall that Wallace had observed a Generation X and Y *"inheritance of absolutely nothing as far as meaningful moral values."* Social capital is **all about** leaving an inheritance of meaningful values and service to family, community, and society-at-large.

Therefore, Deep Wealth necessitates being challenged on deeply held beliefs. Challenged to re-think what is really important. Challenged to envision new ways of living. Why? Because just as it matters what goals you have, it also matters what values you have and what story you are living. As we've alluded to here, some stories are better than others.

All of the historical examples of great leaders and meaningful change were brought about by those who lived out a story that was true. "True" means the story was consistent with the human condition. Social capital is dependent on things like character, virtue, integrity, trust, and service. Those qualities are only successfully integrated into society through individuals galvanized and inspired by the right stories.

So, now let's consider the elements of a good story.

All good stories involve a character we like for some reason. She is doing something good/admirable and we are engaged at this point. The great stories almost always involve a sacrifice on the part of the protagonist... sometimes her own life is at stake. But there is a huge potential reward – an abundance of social capital – that stands to be gained. A person's life, a great cause, or the hope of a nation may be won by the character's valiant effort.

Lincoln's story was compelling because the hope of the nation was at stake. In service of this greater cause, he willingly and repeatedly sacrificed his own interests. His grace helped redeem and restore the Union in the process.

Martin Luther King compelled us because he too embodied grace and service. For a great cause – namely the American Civil Rights Movement – he also sacrificed and suffered. Like Lincoln, he served a cause much bigger than himself and was able to bring about a great redemption of society.

These stories (and countless others like them) are instructive because they point to one central story. What is it that makes these stories so intriguing and inspiring and how can we start to write them into our own lives?

I would submit that there is one ultimate epic tale, one meta-narrative that informs and instructs us. It is the story of Jesus Christ that is the baseline narrative which perfectly presents both the problem and the solution for humanity.

Joseph Campbell, the late scholar and expert of world mythology, explained it this way:[28]

> *"the sign of the cross has to be looked upon as a sign of an eternal affirmation of all that ever was or shall ever be. It symbolizes not only the one historic moment on Calvary but the mystery through all time and space of God's presence and participation in the agony of all living things."*

Christian spirituality teaches that God took on a physical human body in the person of Jesus Christ. The Creator entered into creation. The God of an eternal, timeless realm entered into time. The God who is omnipresent (everywhere) entered into a specific place. He went from being seated on a throne to being born in a barn. He was once surrounded by angels in glory and came into a place where he was disrespected and abused. God who was living in heaven was then living in poverty on earth. He suffered the worst injustice; being without fault, he was tortured and killed under false pretenses. But through his willing sacrifice, he offers hope and redemption to humanity.

Ernest Gordon, a prisoner of war in a Japanese camp during World War II, wrote a book about his POW experience called *Through the Valley of the Kwai.*[29] In the book, Gordon recounts one story of self-sacrifice that is particularly stirring. The POWs had been set to work on a railroad through the jungle. They were working in inhumane conditions - overbearing heat, low food rations, and harsh work hours.

One day, after the POWs had finished an exhaustive day of work on a railroad, their shovels and tools were gathered and counted by the prison guards. Abruptly, the POWs were lined up and a Japanese guard angrily informed them that one of the shovels was missing... One of the men must have stolen it. Since it could be used as a means of escape or sold to the Thais, a stolen shovel was a grave offense. After a long tirade, the guard demanded that the culprit step forward.

No one did.

So the guard, even more enraged, threatened the entire group, shouting "All die! All die!" He pointed a rifle at the first man in the lineup, ready to follow through on his threat.

A POW stepped forward calmly and said that he had done it.

Furious, the guard punched the prisoner repeatedly. The prisoner did not fight back but remained silent. The guard then took the butt of his rifle and rammed it repeatedly onto the prisoner's head. Even after the POW was dead, the guard continued to beat his body. Then he dismissed the POWs to their living quarters.

At the guardhouse, the tools were recounted. They had miscounted; no shovel was missing.

The other POWs who witnessed that murder would never be the same. Each of them undoubtedly understood that, except for the courage and ultimate sacrifice made by their fellow inmate, they may not be alive. They understood the redemptive power of self-sacrifice. They entered into the Christ story. Like that prisoner, Christ was tortured and killed for a false and unjustified accusation. Unlike the ancient gods, Christ is not a god who demands blood, but one who offers his own.

Napoleon distinguished the Christ-story from all the rest when he famously said:

> *"I know men and I tell you that Jesus Christ is no mere man. Between Him and every other person in the world there is no possible term of comparison. Alexander, Caesar, Charlemagne, and I*

> *have founded empires. But on what did we rest the creation of our genius? Upon force. Jesus Christ founded His empire upon love; and at this hour millions of men would die for him."*

There is true peace that comes with embracing this story. Again I will reference Martin Luther King who perfectly illustrated this incredible peace which transcends circumstances in his last speech on April 3, 1968. It's chilling to realize he said these words the night before he was assassinated:[30]

> *"Like anybody, I would like to live a long life. Longevity has its place. But I'm not concerned about that now. I just want to do God's will. And He's allowed me to go up to the mountain. And I've looked over. And I've seen the Promised Land. I may not get there with you. But I want you to know tonight, that we, as a people, will get to the promised land! And so I'm happy tonight. I'm not worried about anything. I'm not fearing any man! Mine eyes have seen the glory of the coming of the Lord!!"*

[7]

Servant Leader

Now we have come full circle and arrived at another "type of soil" or money personality type. You will recall the four money types from Section II: The Mogul, The Star, The Guardian, and The Pleasure Seeker. We now have a fifth type; an entirely different creation called The Servant Leader.

It is crucial to note that the Servant Leader is not like the other soil types. It does not innately characterize anyone. We are not born with it, but aspire toward it. It is something that can be strived for, longed for, and at times embodied.

Still, as previously mentioned, each of us is intrinsically aligned with one of the four soil types, and we will always tend to gravitate back toward one of those. And "cultivating the soil" (through gratitude, contentment, and generosity) is a crucial practice.

However, the Servant Leader is not the result of mere cultivation. Instead, it occurs through an alteration of the soil properties themselves. In other words, the Servant Leader is the result of an inner transformation.

The Servant Leader is characterized by having extensive spiritual capital. In other words, he/she will seem almost impervious to circumstances. There is a deep-seated peace that results in unshakeable conviction and confidence. But it's important to note the confidence is not so much confidence in oneself as it is a confidence rooted in the belief that what is most important can never be taken away. MLK betrayed this type of confidence when he stated emphatically, "I'm not worried about anything. I'm not fearing any man!" As we considered earlier, each of us has a spiritual master which directs us and in which our identity is "rooted."

When that spiritual master is Jesus Christ, one who defeated even death, there is no longer the need to capitulate to anyone or anything. There is an extreme freedom and boldness witnessed in those who have centered their very being on Christ.

At the same time, it is a confidence characterized by humility. It's somewhat paradoxical since we normally think of conviction and confidence as opposites to humility. This is an unusual but extremely powerful combination in practice. In fact, it is the exact combination of character traits – will and humility – which Jim Collins identified as Level 5 Leaders in *Good to Great.* It is the almost paradoxical combination of boldness and humility.

Toward the conclusion of his book, Collins concluded:[31]

> *"(I)n the end, it is impossible to have a great life unless it is a meaningful life. And it is very difficult to have a meaningful life without meaningful work. Perhaps, then, you might gain that rare tranquility that comes from knowing that you've had a hand in creating something of intrinsic excellence that makes a contribution. Indeed, you might even gain that deepest of all satisfactions: knowing that your short time here on this earth has been well spent, and that it mattered."*

Collins was saying that "a great life" is contingent on involvement in something much bigger than ourselves and serving the greater good.

Mimi Silbert has more than 18,000 adopted "children" since the founding of the Delancey Street program 30 years ago. That's the number of graduates from her program that provides academic, vocational and social skills to its residents. The residents, by the way, are a rag-tag bunch of society's worst elements: repeat criminals, prostitutes, hardcore drug-addicts, and the homeless. Delancey is headquartered in San Francisco with a handful of other locations across the country.

Silbert often compares Delancey Street to Harvard saying,[32]

> *"They're very snooty about taking the top two percent, and we're equally snooty about finding the bottom two percent."*

Delancey Street is one of those things that would sound crazy if it hadn't worked so well for so long. It's actually a residence where criminals live and work together. Aside from the diminutive Silbert, the criminals run the place themselves.

Delancey Street contains multiple business enterprises, the profits from which support the program along with donations. It accepts no government money. The businesses include an upscale restaurant, a moving company, a bookstore-café, and a print shop. Most of the residents "graduate" and go out on their own into society after a four-year stay. Nearly 60% of those who enter the program make it through and sustain productive lives afterward.

Despite having doctorate degrees in criminology and philosophy from the University of California at Berkley, Silbert claims that her most important ideas were learned through her own life experiences rather than in the classroom.

Much like Gladwell's conclusions from *Outliers*, Silbert believes that an individual's circumstances and surroundings in their formative years have much to do with their plight in life. She said,[33]

> *"You don't realize how many things are handed down through the family. It's an informal process of learning, and if it hasn't been handed down, you haven't learned it. The people who come to Delancey Street have no idea how to live."*

She explained that the founding of Delancey Street materialized as a result of her contemplations with a friend:[34]

> *"(W)e thought, 'Let's pretend that nothing exists and create what common sense – which is in short supply everywhere – would dictate.' And that's what we did. We made the decision to function as a family, because no matter what shape they're in, families persevere and find new ways to regenerate. In a family, people take care of each other."*

Silbert is not naïve about the motives of those who enter the program. Criminals choose to live at Delancey when judges offer it as an alternative to serving time in prison. They view it as a "get out of jail free" pass rather than an opportunity to truly change their lives. Silbert acknowledges:[35]

> *"I know that when these people come here they're not motivated to change... When they come here their goal is to manipulate. And our goal is to manipulate them, to keep them so busy that they don't think about leaving. Everything is geared to get you through the minute. And then the next minute. And then you've stayed a month. And once you've stayed a month, you think, 'What the hell, another month.'"*

Not everyone makes it through the Delancey Street program. Around one-third drop out or get kicked out of the program in the first few months. However, most of them stay because the first few weeks open them up to an astonishing possibility: Their lives could actually take a different course. There's real hope. They see people just like themselves – long-time residents who've lasted two, three, or four years at Delancey - now running its profitable businesses.

[8]

Hope

"I stood on the edge, tied to a noose, but you came along and cut me loose."

– "Amsterdam" by Coldplay [36]

When I think of hope, I often think back to a scene from the movie *Shawshank Redemption*.[37] The two main characters are Andy Dufresne (played by Tim Robbins), a man wrongly sentenced to life in prison for killing his wife and her lover, and "Red" (played by Morgan Freedman), an inmate in his 60's who was also sentenced for life and had been at Shawshank for his entire adulthood.

Red is sitting in the prison cafeteria eating and talking with about eight other inmates. As the men are talking, Andy walks in with his meal and sits down to join them. Andy had just been released from a two week sentence in solitary confinement. As the guys start to ask Andy about his time in the "hole," the subject turns to music. Andy begins to explain that music is one of the few things that even the prison cannot take away from them. It leads to this exchange between Andy and Red:

Andy: ...There are things in this world not carved out of gray stone. (T)here's a small place inside of us they can never lock away, and that place is called hope.

Red: Hope is a dangerous thing. Drive a man insane. It's got no place here. Better get used to that idea.

Andy: Like Brooks did?

Brooks was an elderly man who had been locked up since his youth. When he was finally set free from Shawshank Prison, he had nowhere to go, no one to look for, and no understanding of how to function in a world that was so different than what he was used to on the "inside." Red referred to Brooks as being "institutionalized," meaning he had lost any idea or desire for coping with the world outside of prison.

Throughout the course of the movie Andy and Red had become quite good friends, and it was nearly always an amiable relationship. This exchange was the most emotionally charged one between the two of them. You could feel the tension and it was obvious that Andy had hit a nerve when talking about hope.

You can really empathize with Red's response. He's been locked up for probably at least 30 years now, and there is no end in sight. He knows his friend is sentenced for life and is maybe 40 years old at this point. To hear him talk like this – to feel him "getting his hopes up" – seemed not only futile but harmful.

Red was making the case that to be able to cope with such a dismal existence, you had to be "realistic." The hope he saw in Andy did not square with the reality he had lived for the majority of his life locked up in prison. In Red's mind, if there was any chance of coping with the misery of life in prison, it was to face the harsh reality of living in a world devoid of dreams and hope.

Red believed that hope and reality were completely incongruous. Any hope in Shawshank prison was baseless and a set-up for the inevitable big, devastating retreat back to their grim existence. This essentially echoes Nietzsche's sentiment:[38]

> *"Hope in reality is the worst of all evils because it prolongs the torments of man."*

Andy, on the other hand, was clearly given strength through his hope. His reference to Brooks was an apt one and it really stung Red to hear it. Brooks was a clear example of what happens when someone finally is set free from prison, but has no real hope or vision of a future outside. Brooks had planned on dying in prison. It was comfortable for him and it was all he knew. With no hope, his newly gained freedom meant nothing.

But what does it even mean to have hope? Our most common understanding of the word connotes great uncertainty. Hope is often thought of as something that, while it would be great if it happened, we wouldn't bank on. It's often even thought of as being disconnected from reality. This is not the correct connotation of the word in the Biblical context. Real hope is not sunny optimism or wishful thinking.

Real hope connotes a confident expectation of a "believed-in future." It is a vision of a much fuller existence. In the context of Christian Spirituality, hope is completely congruent with reality because of a belief that Jesus Christ died and conquered death and suffering. In the words of the Apostle Paul, author of much of the New Testament, "O death, where is thy sting?" Followers of Christ will have a death-conquering future on which to focus. It is hope, grounded in a reality that transcends circumstances and extends even beyond this life.

Theologian Jurgen Moltmann explained how hope kept him alive in a concentration camp after he was captured as a German war prisoner.[39]

> *"I saw how other men collapsed inwardly, how they gave up all hope, sickening for the lack of it, some of them dying. The same thing almost happened to me. What kept me from it was a rebirth*

> *to a new life thanks to a hope for which there was no evidence at all."*

Moltmann's hope was in Jesus Christ.

That sort of hope – a real hope – is ultimately life-sustaining, as it has the power to transform us from passively acquiescing and accepting defeat to actively responding to it. As Victor Frankl observed:[40]

> *"In the final analysis it becomes clear that the sort of person the prisoner became was the result of an inner decision, and not the result of camp influences alone. Fundamentally, therefore, any man can, even under such circumstances, decide what shall become of him – mentally and spiritually."*

Hope does not only give us peace in a dire situation. It can also lend itself toward selflessness and inexplicable kindness and charity. Because, after all, if we have a hope that is centered on one who has conquered death, self-preservation is not the ultimate objective as it would be if we didn't have any such hope. N.T. Wright asserts:[41]

> *"The resurrection opens up before those who would follow Jesus a new life, a new world. And that new life and world, though they will be fulfilled in the life to come, begin here and now."*

Jesus on the cross is actually him on a tree, the tree of eternal life, and he is the fruit of that tree. If we, too, become the fruit (or what C.S. Lewis called "little Christs"), we will take part in a vast and glorious mission of love and grace that has been permeating humanity for the last two thousand years. We become seeds of fruit that fall to the ground.

Jesus compared the Kingdom of God to a tiny mustard seed. Though barely noticeable to the eye, when properly planted it grows into a tree that overtakes all others. It becomes a place that brings shade to the prisoner, the sick, the drugged-out, the lost, the imprisoned and the unloved of the world. It is a place of comfort, belonging and solidarity.

Benjamin and Rosamund Zander tell a moving story in their book, *The Art of Possibility:*[42]

> *Inscribed on five of the six pillars in the Holocaust Memorial at Quincy Market in Boston are stories that speak of the cruelty and suffering in the camps. The sixth pillar presents a tale of a different sort, about a little girl named Ilse, a childhood friend of Guerda Weissman Kline, in Auschwitz. Guerda remembers that Ilse, who was about six years old at the time found one morning a single raspberry somewhere in the camp. Ilse carried it all day long in a protected place in her pocket, and in the evening, her eyes shining with happiness, she presented it to her friend Guerda on a leaf. 'Imagine a world,' writes Guerda, 'in which your entire possession is one raspberry, and you give it to your friend.'*

My oldest daughter is 6 years old. I cried picturing her as I first read this. The little girl in this story had abundance. Of course, it was not a material abundance. She gave away her one and only possession. But she had something stronger. She had a spiritual abundance; an inner peace and love for her friend that could not be taken away.

Living in the United States in the 21st Century, it is obvious to see that we are obsessed with the notion of freedom. But do we really know what it means? If everything were taken away, would we still be free? Do we have a freedom - *can* we have a freedom – that can never be taken away? That is the abundant life. One that is absolutely impervious to circumstances.

The abundant life is connected to a hope that transcends the present circumstances and envisions a world that is ultimately being redeemed and will one day be restored to what it ought to be. A world in which death, suffering, pain, and loss are undone.

[9]

Living a New Story

Having a true hope by internalizing a vision of God's new creation and the final coming together of heaven and earth will inform our beliefs and encourage us to enter into a whole new story. Entering into a redemptive optimism will stir our desires to subversively scheme of ways to shine a light in the darkness; to initiate instances of grace and love in a broken and embittered world.

In the redemptive story, everything we do **matters**. There is meaning in all things. As N.T. Wright explains:[43]

> *What you do in the Lord is not in vain. You are not oiling the wheels of a machine that's shortly going to roll off a cliff. You are not restoring a great painting that's shortly going to be thrown into the fire. You are not planting roses in a garden that's about to be dug up for a building site. You are – strange as it may seem, almost as hard to believe as the resurrection itself – accomplishing something that will become in due course part of God's new world.*

Every act of love, gratitude, and kindness; every work of art or music inspired by the love of God and delight in the beauty of his creation; every minute spent teaching a severely handicapped child to read or to walk; every act of care and nurture, of comfort and support, for one's fellow human beings and for that matter one's fellow creatures...all of this will find its way, through the resurrecting power of God, into the new creation that God will one day make.

When Mimi Silbert walks the halls of the dorm greeting new residents with a "good morning" greeting, it is not unusual for her to be assaulted with profanity in return. This is a woman who studied under Jean-Paul Sartre in Paris. Instead of teaching in the comfort of an Ivy League school and esteemed by her peers, she has chosen to be surrounded by hardened prisoners who often treat her with disdain. She inspires incredible transformation by challenging them:[44]

"You want to quit? That's what you have always done, given up when it got difficult. If you're too angry and hopeless to fight for yourself, then do it for the next guy."

As a result of her redemptive love, gang members once sworn to kill one another are living peacefully together and working side-by-side dressed in suits and running an upscale restaurant.

Certainly there is evidence of decline in social capital, but there are also sprouts of growth – green shoots – all around us. There are countless examples like those of Delancey Street where things are happening that just aren't supposed to happen.

A term that is being used more frequently is "social entrepreneur." As the author David Bornstein puts it,[45] social entrepreneurs are

"transformative forces: people with new ideas to address major problems who are relentless in the pursuit of their visions, people

who simply will not take 'no' for an answer, who will not give up until they have spread their ideas as far as they possibly can."

Thankfully, there are people everywhere who have refused to take "no" for an answer and have refused to give in to the ever-pervasive cynicism and hopelessness. Instead, they are working to help redeem humanity and renew their communities. All throughout the earth, there are people who are strengthening the social fabric and taking part in the renewal of our world. These are servant leaders who are the good fruit that will continue to multiply.

The challenge before us is to embrace love and hope and reject death and defeat. We can refuse to accept things as they are or always have been and work toward "what ought to be."

Over the last decade, we've witnessed the dangers of wealth like a river drowning both perpetrators and victims alike in a tidal wave of greed, deception, and lawlessness. The fallout from the likes of Enron, Worldcom, Madoff, and Lehman has been severe and enduring. Lest anyone think that success and wealth be measured solely by financial metrics, we should look no further than the tangible loss of trust and public confidence in our economic system since the early 2000's.

And yet, however destructive a river can be, it is ultimately the source of life. Water is meant to flow; not stagnate. Likewise, from a wealth perspective, we are meant to continue to keep our resources in motion. Our time, talent, and money harnessed collectively have the ability to quench the thirst of a barren and dry world. Picture not just a trickle-down effect but all corners of the world awash in a restorative movement to fix what is broken and love those who have been forgotten.

The implication of all of this is the paradox that real financial freedom is found not in independence but interdependence. The reality is we are all part of an ever more complex, more interconnected world, whereby our fate – individually and collectively – is dependent on our ability to serve a higher purpose and love one another.

By doing so, we can start to find real hope and true peace. We can discover Deep Wealth.

Acknowledgments

I spent a decade writing this book. I nearly gave up on it multiple times and surely would have done so had it not been for the unending encouragement and support from my wife, Jennifer.

A number of ideas in this book matured through years of conversations with my friend, Ed Briscoe. He has been one of the few people who "get it" when it comes to integrating faith with work and investing.

I am also thankful to my sister, Erika, who has been a great advocate and sounding board in the creative process of putting these thoughts to paper.

Bob Fragasso gave me my first opportunity to work with a team of financial planners in a collaborative, client-centered culture. And Mark Brown taught me a lot about how to communicate complex solutions to clients with elegant simplicity.

I've had the good fortune to work with a wide range of colleagues who have taught me a great deal, including Justin Cassida, Becky Kennedy, Steve Roberts, John Bock, Matt Blackburn, Matt Logar, Brian Jaros, Chris Bixby, Angela Granata, Tom Jennings, and Joel Redmond. Just to name a few.

Another big influence over the years has been the amazing group of people at Denver Presbyterian Church, who are too numerous to mention. My pastor, Bill Connors, has consistently inspired and challenged me through his teachings over the last five years.

Tim Keller of Redeemer Presbyterian Church in NYC has helped me to see my faith in a whole new light. I have lost count of the many sermons of his I have listened to repeatedly over the years. His messages have transformed my thinking and, undoubtedly, influenced this book in ways I am not even aware.

Two of my biggest influences lived on a different continent and died well before I was born. C. S. Lewis and G. K. Chesterton had ways of clearly articulating things that were the vaguest of thoughts bouncing around my mind. They tied together ideas, concepts, and truths in astounding ways that permanently altered my thinking about life, faith, and relationships. They inspired me; inspired me so much that I just had to find and articulate the link between my vocation and the deeper truths lurking just beneath the surface. And I'm grateful to be able to share those thoughts here.

Appendix

[1]

Money Personality Questionnaire

Strongly Agree	Agree	Neutral	Agree	**Strongly Agree**
2	1	0	1	2
M	M		P	P
☐	☐	☐	☐	☐

I have very little free time because I overcommit

My free time is very important to me

Strongly Agree	Agree	Neutral	Agree	**Strongly Agree**
2	1	0	1	2
P	P		G	G
☐	☐	☐	☐	☐

Money allows me to do to do what I want

Money allows me to feel secure

3	Strongly Agree	Agree	Neutral	Agree	Strongly Agree
	2	1	0	1	2
	G	G		M	M
	☐	☐	☐	☐	☐

I am self-sufficient, self-supporting

I encourage others to be involved

4	Strongly Agree	Agree	Neutral	Agree	Strongly Agree
	2	1	0	1	2
	P	P		S	S
	☐	☐	☐	☐	☐

I feel restricted by making too many plans

I am agreeable to do things other people's way

5	Strongly Agree	Agree	Neutral	Agree	Strongly Agree
	2	1	0	1	2
	S	S		M	M
	☐	☐	☐	☐	☐

I am intensely faithful to friends and colleagues

I am fearless, daring and forward-looking

6	Strongly Agree	Agree	Neutral	Agree	Strongly Agree
	2	1	0	1	2
	P	P		G	G
	☐	☐	☐	☐	☐

I follow my intuition even with big purchase decisions

I do extensive research prior to making any big purchases

7	Strongly Agree	Agree	Neutral	Agree	Strongly Agree
	2	1	0	1	2
	P	P		M	M
	☐	☐	☐	☐	☐

I am easy-going   I am competitive

8	Strongly Agree	Agree	Neutral	Agree	Strongly Agree
	2	1	0	1	2
	G	G		S	S
	☐	☐	☐	☐	☐

I am strong-willed   I avoid confrontation
and opinionated

9	Strongly Agree	Agree	Neutral	Agree	Strongly Agree
	2	1	0	1	2
	S	S		M	M
	☐	☐	☐	☐	☐

I will rationalize a big purchase   I will rationalize a big purchase
by thinking (s)he will love it   as being a good investment

10	Strongly Agree	Agree	Neutral	Agree	Strongly Agree
	2	1	0	1	2
	M	M		G	G
	☐	☐	☐	☐	☐

I fear being viewed as   I fear being humiliated
incompetent or unimportant

11

Strongly Agree	Agree	Neutral	Agree	Strongly Agree
2	1	0	1	2
P	P		S	S
☐	☐	☐	☐	☐

To justify making a purchase I think "it's only money"

To justify making a purchase I think "it's a good deal"

12

Strongly Agree	Agree	Neutral	Agree	Strongly Agree
2	1	0	1	2
P	P		S	S
☐	☐	☐	☐	☐

I tend to mind my own business

I understand what people want and need

13

Strongly Agree	Agree	Neutral	Agree	Strongly Agree
2	1	0	1	2
G	G		M	M
☐	☐	☐	☐	☐

If I came into a lot of money, I would not have to worry

If I came into a lot of money, I would invest it in a business

14

Strongly Agree	Agree	Neutral	Agree	Strongly Agree
2	1	0	1	2
S	S		G	G
☐	☐	☐	☐	☐

I am diplomatic

I am detailed

15	Strongly Agree	Agree	Neutral	Agree	Strongly Agree
	2	1	0	1	2
	M	M		G	G
	☐	☐	☐	☐	☐

If I find that a friend paid less If I find that a friend paid less
I will think: "well, time is money" I think: "I find bargains too"

16	Strongly Agree	Agree	Neutral	Agree	Strongly Agree
	2	1	0	1	2
	P	P		G	G
	☐	☐	☐	☐	☐

Money can free up my time Money can help solve
          many of my problems

17	Strongly Agree	Agree	Neutral	Agree	Strongly Agree
	2	1	0	1	2
	P	P		S	S
	☐	☐	☐	☐	☐

If seldom volunteer   I often volunteer

18	Strongly Agree	Agree	Neutral	Agree	Strongly Agree
	2	1	0	1	2
	M	M		S	S
	☐	☐	☐	☐	☐

Money is a means to an end Money makes relationships
           smoother

19	Strongly Agree	Agree	Neutral	Agree	Strongly Agree
	2	1	0	1	2
	M	M		S	S
	☐	☐	☐	☐	☐

I am inspiring, motivating   I am accommodating, willing to please

20	Strongly Agree	Agree	Neutral	Agree	Strongly Agree
	2	1	0	1	2
	S	S		P	P
	☐	☐	☐	☐	☐

When asked to do something I don't have time for, I say yes in order to help out

When asked to do something I don't have time for, I say no because time is too precious

Scoring Instructions:

Every answer receives a score of 0, 1, or 2 points.

If the middle box ("neutral") is checked, the score for that question is zero.

For every 1 or 2 point score, there is a letter just above the box that corresponds to it. The letters are P, G, M, and S. For each question you will want to register a score for the appropriate letter.

- If the box directly to the left or right of neutral is checked, the score is 1 for that letter.
- If the box on the far left or far right is checked, the score is 2 for that letter.

KEY – The final assessment of your own money personality type will be based on which the following four types scored the most points.

Pleasure-Seeker (Total of all points corresponding to the letter 'P')

Guardian (Total of all points corresponding to the letter 'G')

Mogul (Total of all points corresponding to the letter 'M')

Star (Total of all points corresponding to the letter 'S')

[2]

Advanced Estate Planning

Excess Wealth

In the process of completing the Retirement Scorecard, you should have identified whether you have sufficient wealth to achieve your financial goals. We'll call this your "core wealth". Anything you have beyond your "core wealth" is "excess wealth". There are really only three options for any excess wealth you may have:

1) Children
2) Charities
3) Government

Gifting to Children and Grandchildren

There are several key factors to consider with regard to wealth transfers to children:

- Timing – Gifting during lifetime vs. after you pass away
- Education – Preparing heirs for inheritance
- Stipulations – Incorporating provisions in trust to dictate when to make payments

When considering the ideal timing of gifts to children, you'll want to consider when they might have the greatest need for financial assistance. However, you'll also want to balance that consideration with their financial acumen and ability to properly manage money. The annual gift tax exclusion allows you to give up to $14,000 per person without any federal gift tax consequences. An annual gifting program is a great way to systematically distribute portions of your estate gift tax free. It is particularly effective for appreciating assets (like business interest, stocks, or real estate with significant upside potential).

It is important to note that you can engage in this type of lifetime gifting plan, but still avoid gifting directly to children. So, for instance, if you are worried about the fiscal responsibility of children, you can make annual gifts to a trust or to fund an insurance policy for their benefit. That allows you to control the timing and terms of distribution to the children but still take advantage of the annual gift exclusion.

If your current estate plan dictates that funds will be in trust for the benefit of your heirs and you are worried that a future inheritance may act as a disincentive for your beneficiaries to work and be productive, you can incorporate incentive language into your trust document(s). It can provide financial incentives for beneficiaries to pursue certain goals you want to encourage (i.e., matching a salary, engaging in philanthropy, helping to fund the start of a business).

Warren Buffett has famously said,

> *"I want to give my children enough money so that they can do anything, but not so much so that they can do nothing."*

Given the potential for entitlement or apathy that Buffett is pointing out, it's really important to consider at the onset of developing an estate planning strategy whether you have a specific limitation in mind for how much you'd want to pass on to your heirs. If you do have a "cap" to that gifting, it is important to proactively plan so that anything beyond that amount will go to philanthropic causes to the extent you desire and can afford.

Philanthropy and Charitable Giving

The easiest and most straightforward way to make a charitable gift is to name certain charities and amounts in your will or trust. These are referred to as "outright bequests" and are especially appropriate when the gift is relatively small or you want the funds to pass to a charity without any strings attached.

If you have highly appreciated assets like shares of stock, you should consider gifting those directly to charity rather than cash. When you gift appreciated stock, you receive an immediate income tax deduction for the full market value of the donated shares. You will also avoid paying capital gains taxes that you would have otherwise paid if you sold the stock and then gave the cash to charity.

Charitable Trusts

Charitable Trusts are a way to support both a charitable and a non-charitable beneficiary. There are two types of charitable trusts – charitable remainder trusts and charitable lead trusts – which are mirror images of one another. These types of trusts split their interest between two types of beneficiaries: income beneficiary and remainder beneficiary. The names signify the timing of the payments to charities.

Charitable lead trusts (CLTs) provide payments to your designated charitable organization(s) at least annually. When the trust term ends, the remaining trust assets pass to the non-charitable beneficiary (often a child or grandchild). A CLT is most appropriate when you do not need additional income for your own financial independence and can work really well if you are able to fund it with assets that you expect to substantially appreciate in value.

Charitable remainder trusts (CRTs) provide you and/or your spouse income payments (at least annually) for a period of years (often your lifespan). At the end of the payment period (or when you pass away), the assets pass to the charitable organization(s) that you have named. A CRT is most effective in situations where have an appreciated asset with a low cost basis to fund it (capital gains taxes are avoided on sales of assets in a CRT), and you need an additional stream of income to fund your financial independence.

Private Foundations

These are no longer just a tool for the ultra-wealthy. Many of the clients I work with are business owners who are setting up private foundations. These are social entrepreneurs in the mode of Bill Gates (but on a much scaled back version) whereby their ingenuity is applied to the public sector to create a real impact in the community and leave a legacy in an area in which they are passionate. Also, for many business owners, they are disappointed when their children are not willing or able to take over the family business. However, foundations can be a way to create that interfamily enterprise and even allow the opportunity to hire family members to serve on the board.

Foundations are the only estate planning tool that allows parents to observe their children's ability to manage money firsthand. How well young adults manage foundation finances can be a yardstick for how they'll handle any future inheritance.

Donor-Advised Funds

An alternative to creating a private foundation or giving directly to a charity is a donor-advised fund. Donor-advised funds are charitable giving vehicles typically administered by public charities and created in order to manage charitable donations on behalf of a family or individual. You can receive an immediate tax deduction of up to five years' worth of charitable deductions in one year. Donor-advised funds can also be appealing because they are easy to establish and administer and less costly than private foundations. However, they do not offer the level of flexibility and control of private foundations and, unlike foundations, are limited to making grants to public charities.

Life Insurance and Estate Planning

As we mentioned earlier, life insurance can serve a number of traditional purposes such as providing income to survivors, provide for your children's education, paying off a mortgage, and funeral expenses. However, life insurance can also be used for a number of estate planning purposes such as providing sufficient estate liquidity, facilitating a more equal distribution of wealth transferred to heirs, and to replace wealth lost due to the expenses and taxes that may follow your death.

Taxes can greatly reduce the life insurance benefits that your family actually receives if you fail to plan properly. While life insurance proceeds are generally income-tax free to beneficiaries, there can be other estate-related taxes due if not title properly. Often, it is best to own life insurance in an irrevocable life insurance trust (ILIT). An ILIT is a trust that is funded, at least in part, by life insurance policies or proceeds. It is an effective estate planning tool that, if properly structured, may help avoid generation-skipping transfer, gift, and estate taxes, while providing a source of liquid funds to your estate for the payment of taxes, debts, and expenses.

Sufficient life insurance coverage owned within an ILIT is particularly important for people with significant illiquid assets like business interest and real estate. Life insurance – particularly if it is owned properly and not part of the taxable estate – can provide sufficient liquidity to ensure that the desired estate plan is able to be carried out without having to sell illiquid assets at depressed values.

Also, many business owners face a big challenge in trying to treat children equally for purposes of an inheritance, but still trying to pass on the business to the one(s) who is interested and capable of running it or working in it. Life insurance owned in an ILIT is one common way to equalize the estate distributions or, if equalization is not the preferred route, at least there can be more options available as to how to have more control over the transfers to different children.

[3]

Retirement Scorecard – Sample & Table of Multipliers

Retirement Scorecard (Sample)

Basic Assumptions

1	Inflation Assumption	3%
2	Return Assumption	7%
3	Years Until Retirement	10

Income and Expenses

		Now	Multiplier	At Retirement
4	Annual Expenses	$60,000	1.34	$80,635
	Look up Inflation Multiplier (#1 and #3)			
5	Annual Income In Retirement (input below)			
	a) Work			
	b) Pensions			$10,000
	c) Social Security			$24,000
	d) Real Estate			
	e) Gifts			
	f) Other			
	TOTAL ('a' through 'f' above)			**$34,000**
6	Net Income Needed From Portfolio			$46,635
	Expenses (#4) minus TOTAL Income (#5)			
7	Adjust Income Need (above) to Account for Taxes			$58,294
	Multiply #6 by 1.25% (assuming 25% effective rate)			

Investments

		Now	Multiplier	At Retirement
8	Investment Assets (Total)	$500,000	1.97	$983,576
	Look up ROR Multiplier (#2 and #3)			
9	Annual Savings	$15,000	15.78	$236,754
	Look up Savings Multiplier (#2 and #3)			
10	Projected Total Investments at Retirement			$1,220,330
	Add #8 and #9			

Evaluation

11	Withdrawal Rate		**4.8%**
	Total Income Needed (#7) / Total Investments (#10)		
12	Score		**C**

If withdrawal rate is below 3.0%:	A (consider gifting & tax planning for excess wealth)
If withdrawal rate ranges from 3-4%:	B (likely a stable & sustainable plan)
If withdrawal rate ranges from 4-5%:	C (continue to monitor & strive for lower end of range)
If withdrawal rate ranges from 5-6%:	D (unlikely to meet your goals; reassess)
If withdrawal rate is above 6%:	F (unsustainable for long term; revisit assumptions)

Table of "Multipliers" (to be used for the Retirement Scorecard)

Years Until Retirement	Inflation Multipliers		Rate of Return Multipliers			Savings Multipliers		
	3%	4%	6%	7%	8%	6%	7%	8%
0	1.0	1.0	1.0	1.0	1.0	1.0	1.0	1.0
1	1.0	1.0	1.1	1.1	1.1	2.1	2.1	2.1
2	1.1	1.1	1.1	1.1	1.2	3.2	3.2	3.2
3	1.1	1.1	1.2	1.2	1.3	4.4	4.4	4.5
4	1.1	1.2	1.3	1.3	1.4	5.6	5.8	5.9
5	1.2	1.2	1.3	1.4	1.5	7.0	7.2	7.3
6	1.2	1.3	1.4	1.5	1.6	8.4	8.7	8.9
7	1.2	1.3	1.5	1.6	1.7	9.9	10.3	10.6
8	1.3	1.4	1.6	1.7	1.9	11.5	12.0	12.5
9	1.3	1.4	1.7	1.8	2.0	13.2	13.8	14.5
10	1.3	1.5	1.8	2.0	2.2	15.0	15.8	16.6
11	1.4	1.5	1.9	2.1	2.3	16.9	17.9	19.0
12	1.4	1.6	2.0	2.3	2.5	18.9	20.1	21.5
13	1.5	1.7	2.1	2.4	2.7	21.0	22.6	24.2
14	1.5	1.7	2.3	2.6	2.9	23.3	25.1	27.2
15	1.6	1.8	2.4	2.8	3.2	25.7	27.9	30.3
16	1.6	1.9	2.5	3.0	3.4	28.2	30.8	33.8
17	1.7	1.9	2.7	3.2	3.7	30.9	34.0	37.5
18	1.7	2.0	2.9	3.4	4.0	33.8	37.4	41.4
19	1.8	2.1	3.0	3.6	4.3	36.8	41.0	45.8
20	1.8	2.2	3.2	3.9	4.7	40.0	44.9	50.4
21	1.9	2.3	3.4	4.1	5.0	43.4	49.0	55.5
22	1.9	2.4	3.6	4.4	5.4	47.0	53.4	60.9
23	2.0	2.5	3.8	4.7	5.9	50.8	58.2	66.8
24	2.0	2.6	4.0	5.1	6.3	54.9	63.2	73.1
25	2.1	2.7	4.3	5.4	6.8	59.2	68.7	80.0
26	2.2	2.8	4.5	5.8	7.4	63.7	74.5	87.4
27	2.2	2.9	4.8	6.2	8.0	68.5	80.7	95.3
28	2.3	3.0	5.1	6.6	8.6	73.6	87.3	104.0
29	2.4	3.1	5.4	7.1	9.3	79.1	94.5	113.3
30	2.4	3.2	5.7	7.6	10.1	84.8	102.1	123.3
31	2.5	3.4	6.1	8.1	10.9	90.9	110.2	134.2
32	2.6	3.5	6.5	8.7	11.7	97.3	118.9	146.0
33	2.7	3.6	6.8	9.3	12.7	104.2	128.3	158.6
34	2.7	3.8	7.3	10.0	13.7	111.4	138.2	172.3
35	2.8	3.9	7.7	10.7	14.8	119.1	148.9	187.1
36	2.9	4.1	8.1	11.4	16.0	127.3	160.3	203.1
37	3.0	4.3	8.6	12.2	17.2	135.9	172.6	220.3
38	3.1	4.4	9.2	13.1	18.6	145.1	185.6	238.9
39	3.2	4.6	9.7	14.0	20.1	154.8	199.6	259.1
40	3.3	4.8	10.3	15.0	21.7	165.0	214.6	280.8
41	3.4	5.0	10.9	16.0	23.5	176.0	230.6	304.2
42	3.5	5.2	11.6	17.1	25.3	187.5	247.8	329.6
43	3.6	5.4	12.3	18.3	27.4	199.8	266.1	356.9
44	3.7	5.6	13.0	19.6	29.6	212.7	285.7	386.5
45	3.8	5.8	13.8	21.0	31.9	226.5	306.8	418.4

Notes

Introduction

1 Lewis, C.S. *The Weight of Glory.* 1949. New York: HarperCollins Publishers, 2001.

2 Dalbar *Quantitative Analysis of Investor Behavior (20ᵗʰ Ed.).* Boston, 2014.

3 Block, Peter. *Stewardship: Choosing Service Over Self Interest.* San Francisco: Berrett-Koehler Publishers, 1993.

4 Corbin, Kenneth. "New Plan: Retirees Want a Post-Career," *On-WallStreet* (6/5/2014).

5 Corbin, Kenneth. "New Plan: Retirees Want a Post-Career," *On-WallStreet* (6/5/2014).

6 Sinek, Simon. *Start with Why: How Great Leaders Inspire Everyone to Take Action.* New York: Penguin Group, 2009.

Section 1 – Human Capital

1 Gladwell, Malcolm. *The Tipping Point: How Little Things Can Make a Big Difference.* Boston: Little, Brown, 2000.

2 Allen, James. *As a Man Thinketh.* 1902. New York: Penguin Group, 2008.

3 Ramachandran, V.S. *Phantoms in the Brain.* New York: HarperCollins Publishers, 1998.

4 Kroger, W.S. *Clinical and Experimental Hypnosis.* 1963. Philadephia: Lippincott Williams & Wilkins, 2008.

5 Frankl, Victor E. *Man's Search for Meaning: An Introduction to Logotherapy.* New York: Simon & Schuster, 1984.

6 Engel, George L., "Sudden and Rapid Death During Psychological Stress," *Annals of Internal Medicine,* vol. 74, 1971, p. 771-782.

7 Cron, Lisa. *Wired for Story: The Writer's Guide to Using Brain Science to Hook Readers from the Very First Sentence.* New York: Crown Publishing Group, 2012.

8 Harrison, Lawrence E. & Huntingdon, Samuel P. *Culture Matters: How Values Shape Human Progress.* New York: Basic Books, 2000.

9 Maddison, Angus. *Contours of the World Economy 1-2030 AD: Essays in Macro-Economic History.* New York: Oxford University Press, 2007.

10 Thoreau, Henry David. *Walden.* Michigan: George Routledge & Sons, 1904.

11 Baumol, William J. *The Free-Market Innovation Machine: Analyzing the Growth Miracle of Capitalism.* New Jersey: Princeton University Press, 2002.

12 The World Bank, *The Changing Wealth of Nations: Measuring Sustainable Development in the New Millenium.* Washington, D.C., 2011.

13 Collins, Jim & Porra, Jerry. *Built to Last: Successful Habits of Visionary Companies.* New York: HarperCollins Publishers, 1994.

14 Sisodia, Raj & Wolfe David B. & Sheth, Jag. *Firms of Endearment: How World-Class Companies Profit from Passion & Purpose.* New Jersey: Wharton School Publishing, 2007.

15 Stengel, Jim. *Grow: How Ideals Power Growth & Profit at the World's Greatest Companies.* New York: Crown Publishing Group, 2011.

16 Spence, Roy M., Jr. *It's Not What You Sell, It's What You Stand For.* New York: Penguin Group, 2009.

17 Spence, Roy M., Jr. *It's Not What You Sell, It's What You Stand For.* New York: Penguin Group, 2009.

18 Sayers, Dorothy L. "Why Work," *Letters to a Diminished Church: Passionate Arguments for the Relevance of Christian Doctrine.* 1942. Nashville, TN: Thomas Nelson, 2004.

19 Csikszentmihalyi, Mihaly. *Flow: The Psychology of Optimal Experience.* New York: Harper & Row, 1990.

20 Twain, Mark. *Adventures of Huckleberry Finn.* 1884. New York: Random House, 1996.

21 Covey, Stephen R. *The 3rd Alternative: Solving Life's Most Difficult Problems.* New York: Free Press, 2012.

22 Anthony, Mitch. *The New Retirementality: Planning Your Life and Living Your Dreams...at Any Age You Want.* New Jersey: John Wiley & Sons, 2008.

23 Freedman, Marc. *Encore: Finding What That Matters in the Second Half of Life.* New York: PublicAffairs Books, 2007.

24 Pascal, Blaise. *Pascal's Pensees.* South Carolina: CreateSpace Independent Publishing, 2013.

25 Freedman, Marc. *Encore: Finding What That Matters in the Second Half of Life.* New York: PublicAffairs Books, 2007.

26 Covey, Stephen R. *The 7 Habits of Highly Effective People: Restoring the Character Ethic.* 1989. New York: Free Press, 2004.

27 O'Kelly, Eugene. *Chasing Daylight: How My Forthcoming Death Transformed My Life.* New York: McGraw-Hill, 2008.

28 Kinder, George. *The Seven Stages of Money Maturity: Understanding the Spirit and Value of Money in Your Life.* New York: Dell Publishing, 1999.

29 Nouwen, Henri. *Making All Things New: An Invitation to the Spiritual Life.* 1981. California: HarperOne, 2009.

30 Schwartz, Barry. *The Paradox of Choice: Why More is Less.* New York: HarperCollins, 2004.

31 Aquinas, Thomas. *Summa Theologiae.* 1265-1274.

32 Frankl, Victor E. *Man's Search for Meaning: An Introduction to Logotherapy.* New York: Simon & Schuster, 1984.

Section 2 – Spiritual Capital

1 Frankl, Victor E. *Man's Search for Meaning: An Introduction to Logotherapy.* New York: Simon & Schuster, 1984.

2 The Holy Bible, *Philippians 4:7 English Standard Version (ESV).* Illinois: Crossway Bibles, 2001.

3 "10 Greatest Actors of All Time," *World Top Rankings and Information.* http://world-top-10.com.

4 Crowther, Linnea. "Marlon Brando: Bad and Brilliant," *Legends and Legacies.* Illinois: Legacy.com, 2012.

5 Litt, Jerome. "Marlon Brando was a Binge Eater," *Psychology Today.* New York: Sussex Publishers, 2009.

6 Boteach, Shmuley. *Kosher Sex: A Recipe for Passion and Intimacy.* New York: Crown Publishing, 2000.

7 *The Wild One*, directed by Laslo Benedek, screenplay by John Paxton, (California: Columbia Pictures, 1953)

8 O'Neill, Jessie H. *The Golden Ghetto: The Psychology of Affluence.* Wisconsin: The Affluenza Project, 1997.

9 Guinness, Os. *The Call: Finding and Fulfilling the Central Purpose of Your Life.* Tennessee: W Publishing Group, 1998.

10 Needleman, Jacob. *Money and the Meaning of Life.* New York: Doubleday/Currency, 1994.

11 Needleman, Jacob. *Money and the Meaning of Life.* New York: Doubleday/Currency, 1994.

12 Lewis, C.S. *Mere Christianity.* New York: HarperCollins, 1952.

13 Taleb, Nassim. *Fooled by Randomness: The Hidden Role of Chance in Life and in the Markets.* New York: Random House, 2004.

14 Glassman, Eric M. *Congressional Gold Medals, 1776-2014.* Washington, D.C.: Congressional Research Office, 2014.

15 Guinness, Os. *The Call: Finding and Fulfilling the Central Purpose of Your Life.* Tennessee: W Publishing Group, 1998.

16 Carnegie, Andrew. *The Gospel of Wealth, and Other Timely Essays.* New York: The Century Co., 1901.

17 Guinness, Os. *The Call: Finding and Fulfilling the Central Purpose of Your Life.* Tennessee: W Publishing Group, 1998.

18 Nasaw, David. *Andrew Carnegie.* New York: The Penguin Group, 2006.

19 Nasaw, David. *Andrew Carnegie.* New York: The Penguin Group, 2006.

20 Mackay, James. *Andrew Carnegie: Little Boss.* Edinburgh: Mainstream Publishing, 1997

21 Keller, Timothy. *Counterfeit Gods: The Empty Promises of Money, Sex, and Power, and the Only Hope that Matters.* New York: Dutton, 2009.

22 Bogle, John C. Enough: *True Measures of Money, Business, and Life.* New Jersey: John Wiley & Sons, 2009.

23 Easterbrook, Gregg. *The Progress Paradox: How Life Gets Better While People Feel Worse.* New York: Random House, 2003.

24 Boethius, *The Consolation of Philosophy: With an Introduction and Contemporary Criticism.* San Francisco: Ignatius Press, 2012.

25 Schwartz, Barry. *The Paradox of Choice: Why More is Less.* New York: HarperCollins, 2004.

26 Kierkegaard, Soren. *Sickness Unto Death.* New York: Penguin Books Limited, 1989.

27 Holowchak, Andrew, M. *Freud: From Individual Psychology to Group Psychology.* Maryland: Jason Aronson, 2012.

28 Becker, Earnest. *The Denial of Death.* New York: The Free Press, 1973.

29 Dylan, Bob. "Gotta Serve Somebody," *Slow Train Coming.* Columbia Records, 1979.

Section 3 – Financial Capital

1 Sier, Ronald. "Why People Don't Want Your Financial Planning Service and It's Not Because They Don't Want You Need, Don't Trust You, Or Don't Believe You," *See Beyond Numbers.* http://seebeyondnumbers.com, November 9, 2013.

2 Sier, Ronald. "Why People Don't Want Your Financial Planning Service and It's Not Because They Don't Want You Need, Don't Trust You, Or Don't Believe You," *See Beyond Numbers.* http://seebeyondnumbers.com, November 9, 2013.

3 Chesterton, G.K. *Orthodoxy.* 1908. New York: Cosimo, 2007.

Section 4 – Social Capital

1 Gladwell, Malcolm. *Outliers: The Story of Success.* New York: Little, Brown & Co., 2008.

2 Guinness, Os. *The Call: Finding and Fulfilling the Central Purpose of Your Life.* Tennessee: W Publishing Group, 1998.

3 Carnegie, Andrew. *The Gospel of Wealth, and Other Timely Essays.* New York: The Century Co., 1901.

4 Field, John. *Social Capital.* Massachusetts: Psychology Press, 2003.

5 Halpern, David. Social Capital. Massachusetts: Polity Press, 2005.

6 Becker, Earnest. *The Denial of Death.* New York: The Free Press, 1973.

7 Plantinga, Cornelius, Jr. *Not the Way It's Supposed to Be: A Breviary of Sin.* Michigan: Wm. B. Eerdmans Publishing, 1995.

8 Putnam, Robert D. *Bowling Along: The Collapse and Revival of American Community.* New York: Simon & Schuster, 2000.

9 Noonan, Peggy. "A Life's Lesson," *The Wall Street Journal.* (6/8/2008).

10 VanderMey, Anne. "Harvard's MBA Oath Goes Viral," *BloombergBusinessweek.* (6/11/2009).

11 Roberts, Mark D. (2009, June 5). "Final Comments on the MBA Oath." Retrieved from http://markdroberts.com/?p=860.

12 Brooks, David. "The Organization Kid," *The Atlantic.* (4/4/2001).

13 Brooks, David. "The Organization Kid," *The Atlantic.* (4/4/2001).

14 Goodwin, Doris Kearns. *Team of Rivals: The Political Genius of Abraham Lincoln.* New York: Simon and Schuster, 2006.

15 Goodwin, Doris Kearns. *Team of Rivals: The Political Genius of Abraham Lincoln.* New York: Simon and Schuster, 2006.

16 Chesterton, G.K. *Orthodoxy.* 1908. New York: Cosimo, 2007.

17 O'Connor, Flannery. *Collected Works.* Page 949. New York: Library of America, 1988.

18 Taylor, Daniel. *The Myth of Certainty: The Reflective Christian & the Risk of Commitment.* Illinois: InterVarsity Press, 1999.

19 *Good Will Hunting,* directed by Gus Van Sant, screenplay by Matt Damon & Ben Affleck. California: Miramax Home Entertainment, 1997

20 Lamott, Anne. *Traveling Mercies: Some Thoughts on Faith.* New York: Anchor Books, 1999.

21 King, Martin Luther, Jr. *Strength to Love.* Ohio: Fortress Press, 1981.

22 Delbanco, Andrew. *The Real American Dream: A Meditation on Hope.* Massachusetts: President & Fellows of Harvard College, 1999.

23 Miller, Donald. A Million Miles in a Thousand Years: What I Learned While Editing My Life. Nashville: Thomas Nelson, 2009.

24 Miller, Laura. "David Foster Wallace," *Salon.* (3/9/1996).

25 McKee, Robert. *Story: Style, Structure, Substance, and the Principles of Screenwriting.* New York: HarperCollins, 1997.

26 Miller, Laura. "David Foster Wallace," *Salon.* (3/9/1996).

27 Dreyfus, Hubert & Kelly, Sean Dorrance. *All Things Shining: Reading the Western Classics to Find Meaning in a Secular Age.* New York: Free Press, 2011.

28 Campbell, Joseph & Moyers, Bill. The Power of Myth. New York: Doubleday, 1988.

29 Gordon, Ernest. *Through the Valley of the Kwai: From Death Camp Despair to Spiritual Triumph.* Oregon: Wipf & Stock Publishers, 1997.

30 King, Martin Luther, Jr. "I've Been to the Mountaintop," delivered in Memphis, Tennessee – April 3, 1968. *Say It Plain: A Century of Great African American Speeches.* By American RadioWorks.

31 Collins, Jim. *Good to Great: Why Some Companies Make the Leap...And Others Don't.* New York: HarperCollins, 2001.

32-35 "Delancey Street: Where Drug Addicts, Criminals, and the Homeless Go to Turn Their Lives Around," *Biography.* New York: A&E Television, August, 1997.

36 Coldplay. "Amsterdam," *Parachutes.* Parlophone, July 2000.

37 *Shawshank Redemption,* directed by Frank Darabont, screenplay by Frank Darabont. California: Castle Rock Entertainment, 1994.

38 Nietzsche, Friedrich. *Human, All Too Human: A Book for Free Spirits.* New York: Cambridge University Press, 1986.

39 Moltmann, Jurgen. *The Crucified God: The Cross of Christ as the Foundation and Criticism of Christian Theology.* 1974. New York: HarperCollins, 1991.

40 Frankl, Victor E. *Man's Search for Meaning: An Introduction to Logotherapy.* New York: Simon & Schuster, 1984.

41 Wright, N. T. *Following Jesus: Biblical Reflections on Discipleship.* London: SPCK, 1994.

42 Zander, Rosamund & Benjamin. *The Art of Possibility.* Massachusetts: Harvard Business School Press, 2000.

43 Wright, N.T. *Surprised By Hope: Rethinking Heaven, the Resurrection, and the Mission of the Church.* New York: HarperCollins, 2008.

44 Whittemore, Hank. "Hitting the Bottom Can Be the Beginning," *Parade Magazine.* (3/15/1992).

45 Bornstein, David & Davis, Susan. *Social Entrepreneurship: What Everyone Needs to Know.* Oxford: Oxford University Press, 2010.

71404962R00149

Made in the USA
San Bernardino, CA
15 March 2018